It was the *best*
of sentences,
it was the *worst*
of sentences.

D0047957

a writer's guide to crafting killer sentences

It was the *best* of sentences, it was the *worst* of sentences.

June Casagrande

TEN SPEED PRESS
Berkeley

Published in the United States by Ten Speed Press, an imprint of the
Crown Publishing Group, a division of Random House, Inc., New York.
www.crownpublishing.com
www.tenspeed.com

Ten Speed Press and the Ten Speed Press colophon are registered
trademarks of Random House, Inc.

Library of Congress Cataloging-in-Publication Data
Casagrande, June.
    It was the best of sentences, it was the worst of sentences : a writer's
guide to crafting killer sentences / June Casagrande. — 1st ed.
        p. cm.
    Includes index.
    Summary: "This humorous writing book from grammar columnist
June Casagrande focuses on the sentence as the unit of meaning in
writing, showing writing students and professional writers alike how to
craft bold, effective, reader-serving sentences"—Provided by publisher.
    1. English language—Sentences—Problems, exercises, etc. 2. English
language—Paragraphs—Problems, exercises, etc. 3. English language—
Rhetoric—Problems, exercises, etc. I. Title.
    PE1441.C43 2010
    808'.042076—dc22

                                                    2009040410

ISBN 978-1-58008-740-7

Printed in the United States of America.

Cover design by Nancy Austin
Interior design by Katy Brown

20 19 18 17 16 15

First Edition

For Diane, Jennifer, and Melanie

Contents

Acknowledgments

:::::

Thanks to my agent, Laurie Abkemeier, and to Lisa Westmoreland, Brie Mazurek, my husband, Ted Averi, the members of my women writers' lunch club, the members of my writers' critique group, friend and photographer extraordinaire Stephanie Diani, Dr. Marisa DiPietro, and the copy editors, proofreaders, designers, and others who worked behind the scenes on this book. Thank you, everyone!

The Sentence

THE WRITER'S MOST IMPORTANT TOOL

:::::

This sentence rocks. It's concise. It's powerful. It knows what it wants to say, and it says it in clear, bold terms.

But upon quickly or slowly reading a sentence such as this, in which the writer quite clearly is wanting to make a point regarding various issues pertaining to general written communication, it suddenly becomes more than clear that this is a sentence whose aspirations of rocking have been handily eclipsed in favor of the act of sucking.

We all know bad writing when we see it. Yet recognizing it and understanding it are two very different things. It seems we never take the time to sit down and ask ourselves what exactly makes a sentence like the one in the previous paragraph so terrible. Yes, it's too long. Yes, it's stuffy. But those issues alone don't capture the breadth and depth of its lameness. The problems with this sentence run much deeper. Understanding the issues that plague it—that plague all our writing—requires thought, time, a grounding in grammar, and the energy to stop and look at the writer's guiding question: what am I really trying to say?

On the rare occasions when we endeavor to understand the difference between good and bad sentences, we can find ourselves lost. Surely good sentences have something to do with all that grammar stuff we were supposed to learn in school—the stuff that somehow escaped us and, as a result, has caused us great shame ever since. We remember a teacher saying something about dangling participles. We have vague memories of someone lecturing about active versus passive voice. We know all this business has something to do with subjects and modifiers. But we don't remember the details. So instead of helping us, these terms taunt us. They linger in the back of our minds, making us feel as if good writing is completely beyond our grasp. So we go on writing badly.

We write bad memos, bad term papers, bad novels, bad cover letters, bad query letters, bad advertising copy, bad e-mails, bad book proposals, bad blog entries, bad grant proposals, and bad technical manuals. We crumble under the weight of our own information, at a loss to convey it to the reader in a way that makes sense. We have so much to say. On many levels, we know we're good writers. Maybe even really good. Yet we just can't form our good information into readable, engaging, comprehensible sentences.

Ironically, most of us are perfectly adept at putting our thoughts and experiences into words—as long as those words are coming out of our mouths and not through our keyboards or pens. No one ever shows up at the office on Monday morning and says of Saturday night's Green Day concert, "Before considering whether to madly rush the stage, charging in the direction of an area rapidly

2

transforming itself and its denizens into what could only be described as a rollicking mosh pit, I purchased and thirstily consumed a cola beverage."

No, it's the act of putting it on paper—forming ideas into sentences—that trips us up. That's true partly because some of us are conditioned to fear writing. Unlike when we speak, we usually spend time thinking about what we want to say before we write, so we have more time to worry about it and thus overcomplicate it. What's more, when we write we often have in our heads more information than we can use, and we don't know what to leave out.

But perhaps the biggest reason that our sentences go bad is that, when we sit down to write, someone is missing. Unlike those bull sessions around the watercooler in which we so adeptly tell stories of concerts and cola consumption, when we write we're all alone. The rapt co-workers looking us in the eye and hanging on every word are nowhere to be found. In their place is a shadow of a someone we may have never met and we'd just as soon not think about—someone called the Reader.

Thy Reader, Thy God

If you want to master the art of the sentence, you must first accept a somewhat unpleasant truth—something a lot of writers would rather deny: The Reader is king. You are his servant. You serve the Reader information. You serve the Reader entertainment. You serve the Reader details of your company's recent merger or details of your experiences in drug rehab. In each case, as a writer you're working for the man (or the woman). Only by knowing your place can you do your job well. You have a boss—a fickle, exacting, surprisingly slick one—and you can't ignore him just because he isn't physically reading over your shoulder. Good writing hangs in the balance.

Here's another way to think of this: Your writing is not about you. It's about the Reader. Even when it's quite literally about you—in memoirs, personal essays, first-person accounts—it's not *really* about you.

Ever read a memoir that sounded too self-pitying? Ever read an op-ed that sounded too preachy or self-important? Ever read a memo that sounded smothered in jargon or unnecessary details? Ever read a blog entry that talked about people you've never met as if you'd known them all your life? Those things happened because the writer forgot her place. She forgot that she was working for you and not the other way around. She was unwittingly attempting to get you to work for her. She was trying to get your pity or evoke your shock for her own purposes. She was trying to tell you what to think instead of giving you information from which you could draw your own conclusions. She was focused on the details of her own situation without asking herself which details were relevant to yours.

Readers don't read memoirs because Frank McCourt needs pity or because Jeannette Walls needs you to know that her parents were unstable or because Mary Karr wants to get some stuff off her chest. In each of these memoirists' amazing stories, the Reader finds not just entertainment but themes that touch on his own life—themes of hope, perseverance, suffering, and the power to overcome.

When you forget the Reader, you get what I call writer-serving writing. It exists at every level of writing expertise. I've gagged on it when reading personal essays and caught whiffs of it in

4

award-winning books and articles. I've been horrified to notice it in my own writing. Writer-serving writing is perfectly appropriate in diaries and journals—but any writing that's meant to be seen by a Reader must serve the Reader. If you like, we can make an exception for diary-like blogs in which the Reader is like a voyeur. But that's the exception. This is the rule: whether you're Christian, Jew, Muslim, or a disciple of the church of Penn Jillette, when you sit down to write, the Reader is thy god.

True, you can't know everything the Reader wants. You can't serve all the Readers all the time. And you shouldn't try. But there is one thing all Readers want: clear, concise, comprehensible sentences that mean something to *them*.

Oh, Yes, There Will Be Grammar

This is where grammar comes in. This is where word choice comes in. This is where questions about clarity come in. This is where I come in.

In this book, I hope to share some information I believe can be very helpful to you, my Reader, about the art of sentence writing. I arrived at this information not as a teacher of writing or a critic of great literature. I arrived at it as a student of grammar.

For years I've been writing a column about grammar and style, which in turn spawned two books on the subject and more of the professional copyediting work I had already been doing for years. And in this journey, I stumbled across a truth that no one had told me before. Grammar isn't just a list of pedantic prohibitions. Nor is it just an academic pursuit of labeling parts of speech and analyzing how they work together. Grammar is actually useful. It really can help your writing, as you will see in this book.

Sentenced to Life

Grammar isn't the only key to good sentence writing, of course. Word choice, common sense, passion, information—all these elements and more are essential.

Yet all great writing has one thing in common. It starts with a sentence. The sentence is a microcosm of any written work, and understanding it means understanding writing itself—how to structure ideas, how to emphasize what's important, how to make practical use of grammar, how to cut the bull, and, above all, how to serve the almighty Reader.

If I live up to my goal of serving you well, that's what you'll learn here.

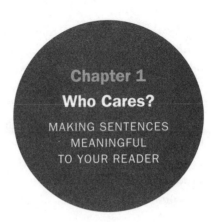

Chapter 1
Who Cares?
MAKING SENTENCES MEANINGFUL TO YOUR READER

For years I made my living schlepping city council stories for a small community newspaper. Perhaps a third of the articles I wrote could have begun with an identical opener: "On Tuesday, the city council voted to . . ." But they didn't. The reason: the almighty Reader.

In any type of writing, be it journalism, fiction, or advertising copy, the almighty Reader is the boss. But there's no better field for understanding this than community news. When I worked in that field, the Reader was always in my face. He wasn't like the silent, invisible, fickle master consuming literary fiction, corporate earnings reports, or sales brochures. The community news Reader wrote to me. He called me. And, because I was working in a much smaller arena than that of big-city reporters, he knew me. The Reader considered me part of the community, even though I lived fifty miles away, and he expected me to serve the town's best interests while answering to him directly.

Yes, this got annoying at times. Especially when he failed to realize that he didn't get to assign me stories: "I want you to do an exposé on how the president of my condo association refuses to put up 'Keep Off the Grass' signs." In community news, the Reader will not be ignored.

Now that I no longer wake up in the middle of the night screaming, "I will not write a front-page article about your dog!" I realize this experience is a good thing. It helped me understand how to form sentences that serve the Reader.

Consider this story lead:

> The city council on Tuesday voted on a budget that contains no funds for fixing Main Street potholes.

Informative, relevant, clear, true. But could the writer do a better job of remembering her boss, the Reader? Absolutely. A sentence like the one just stated is written from a writer's perspective. The writer's job consisted of going to a meeting, documenting a vote, and perhaps listening to some discussion of one important element of that vote—pothole repair. So that's what got emphasized in the sentence.

But this approach downplays the facts that are most pertinent to the Reader. Look at the main subject and action of the sentence: *The city council voted.* The Reader already knows that the council voted. The council is always voting. It votes on thirty, forty, fifty things a month—most of which are total yawners. The Reader doesn't really care that the council voted. He cares about what it all means to him.

These are the questions that a skilled newswriter asks: "How will this affect the Reader? Why should he care?" Such questions lead to an opener like this:

> The bumpy ride on Main Street isn't going to get smoother anytime soon.

Although this example works well, we've all seen this go too far. Used dishonorably, this approach can come off as pandering or even downright sleazy. Nonprint media come to mind: "Something in your kitchen wants to kill your children! Details at eleven."

But if you stop and think about such sleazy tactics, you see that this lead really has the same problem as the snoozer lead: It's writer-serving writing as opposed to Reader-serving or Viewer-serving writing. It's deliberate manipulation, and Viewers can smell it a mile away. It works—but the best writing doesn't stoop to this level.

To strike a balance between snoozer "the city council voted" sentences and sleazy "there's a killer in your kitchen" sentences, all you have to do is remember the Reader. Ask, "What's important to my Reader?" not just, "What will get his attention?"

The answer—be it about the bumpy ride on Main Street or the bottom line on a tax bill—then becomes the main point of your sentence, and your sentence can become a thing of real value.

Of course, it's not always that simple. Wanting to accommodate your Reader and actually pulling it off are two different things. Ironically, sometimes the very act of trying to explain things to the Reader creates problems. Consider this sentence, written by a professional writer, which was in a piece I copyedited. I've disguised it slightly to save the writer embarrassment:

> While the boat show is predictably crowded over the weekends, holding the event over Thanksgiving for the second

> consecutive year positively impacts the flow of attendees over the closing weekend, which is traditionally the busiest.

Any copy editor who works with novice writers sees stuff like this all the time. This sentence, while not the worst ever, contains a number of problems that are all rooted in the writer's misguided attempts to explain stuff to the Reader. Let's look at it piece by piece:

> While the boat show

While is a subordinating conjunction, which we'll talk about in chapter 2. There's nothing wrong with starting a sentence with a subordinating conjunction in general or with *while* in particular. But such an opening can, in unskilled hands, pave the way for a problematic sentence. At the very least, it tells the Reader, "Stay put. It could be a while before I get to the point."

> is predictably crowded

Really? It's *predictably crowded*? We can see what the writer meant: the show is so consistently crowded on the weekends that you could predict it. But does *predictably crowded* really capture this? The adverb *predictably* comes right before the adjective *crowded*, as if it's modifying *crowded*, as if it means that *predictably* is a way—a manner—of being crowded. As you'll see in chapter 7, adverbs are flexible. They're so flexible, in fact, that they can modify whole sentences. You could argue, then, that this part of our sentence is okay. But is it good? No.

> over the weekends

Nothing wrong with that—yet. But two more *over* phrases are about to appear in this sentence, so *over the weekends* sets up an annoying redundancy. We'll look at this type of problem more in chapter 9 when we discuss prepositional phrases.

> holding the event over Thanksgiving for the second consecutive year positively impacts the flow of attendees

Most of the choices reflected in this clause might be fine in certain cases. But the overall effect stinks. For starters, this is the main clause of our sentence. That means it contains our main subject and our main verb. (We'll look at clause structure in chapter 3.) But both are downright anemic. *Holding*—the subject of our lengthy, winding sentence—is a form of a word that usually connotes action: *I hold, you hold, he holds*. But here it's made into something called a gerund, which is basically a noun. We'll talk more about actions made into nouns in chapter 13. The usage is grammatical, but is it wise to make this the main subject? Do you really want the single most important actor in your whole sentence to be the abstract concept of *holding*?

Here's a more troubling part of that excerpt:

> for the second consecutive year

The way this phrase modifies *holding* makes the sentence illogical. Let me pare down the sentence to show you what I mean: *Holding the event for the second consecutive year positively impacts the flow.* See how *for the second consecutive year* attaches itself to *holding*? We're no longer talking about just holding. We're talking specifically about the second time you do it. So our sentence says that the benefits of holding the boat show over Thanksgiving weekend apply only the

11

second year. In years three, four, and five, holding it over Thanksgiving weekend has no effect. Only holding it for the second consecutive year impacts the flow. That's just wrong.

> positively impacts the flow of attendees

Positively impacts sounds like something in a corporate earnings report, and *flow of attendees* sounds like something in a fire safety manual. Each of these phrases squanders an opportunity to connect with the Reader in a more meaningful and tangible way. The Reader knows all about long ticket lines, bottlenecked foot traffic, and crowds in stadiums. He has visual and emotional associations with the concept of crowd control. There are so many ways to make the concept more meaningful than *positively impacts the flow of attendees*.

Impacts, all by itself, is a problem. It couldn't be vaguer. Here it's used to mean that something improves or reduces or ameliorates crowding. But *impacts* contains less information than any of these alternatives. Also, why use a word that could mean something negative *or* positive when you're clearly talking about something positive? (We'll discuss choosing specific words in chapter 6.) Making matters worse, some people argue that *impact* isn't really a verb. They're wrong. But since you'll never get a chance to sit down and explain that to them, you have to decide whether it's worth irking them.

Oh, and don't miss that second *over* phrase,

> over Thanksgiving

because here comes our third *over* phrase:

> over the closing weekend

12

So we now have in one sentence *over the weekends, over Thanksgiving*, and *over the closing weekend*. Personally, I'm amazed that the writer did such a good job of associating each time element with a specific action. Usually when you see this many time elements in a sentence you end up with a nonsensical statement like *He took a three-year hiatus in 1992* or *over the weekend he got lost over the course of three hours*. The three *over* phrases in one sentence tell us that the writer was simply cramming in too much information. Then, as if that weren't enough, one last thought gets tacked on:

which is traditionally the busiest.

This is called a relative clause (which we'll discuss in chapter 8). Relative clauses can be great for squeezing in more information—when the information fits. But the usage here is like squeezing Louie Anderson into Ryan Seacrest's jogging shorts. Not pretty.

Just look at all the distinct pieces of information we have in this sentence:

The boat show is crowded on the weekends.

This crowding is predictable.

The event is being held [or can be held] over Thanksgiving.

The event was held over Thanksgiving last year.

Holding it over Thanksgiving means crowds are better spread out over the duration of the show.

This improves crowding on the closing weekend.

The closing weekend is traditionally the busiest.

We can understand why the writer didn't want to spend too much time on each of those points. But his attempt to slip them in gracefully failed because he was overambitious. He crammed in too much. The best thing you can do in a situation like this is to first consider whether any information can go (I, for one, can do without that *predictably* business) and to then break up what's left into smaller sentences. The possibilities are endless:

> The boat show gets crowded on the weekends. So this year, for the second time, it will conclude over the four-day Thanksgiving weekend. This spreads out the number of visitors and relieves crowding during the closing weekend, which is traditionally the busiest.

or

> Saturdays and Sundays usually mean huge crowds at the boat show. The closing weekend gets especially jammed. But last year the producers had an idea: why not make the last weekend of the event the four-day Thanksgiving weekend? The strategy was so successful at reducing overcrowding that they're doing it again this year.

I could go on. But you get the idea.

As a writer, it's your job to organize information, to prioritize it with the Reader in mind, to chop and add as you see fit. But only by fully understanding the mechanics of the sentence can you do so in the best possible way.

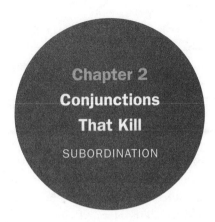

Chapter 2
Conjunctions That Kill
SUBORDINATION

Say, here's a god-awful sentence:

> After walking into the office, retrieving the gun from his desk drawer, shooting his business partner in the face, and quickly beginning to understand that he needed to escape immediately, John realized he was tired.

If you don't see right away what's so terrible about that sentence, read it again, but don't focus on the grammar or the adverbs or even the length. Focus on the meaning. What's the main point? A number of things are happening in this sentence: a man walks into an office, he gets a gun, he shoots his business partner in the face, and he gets that panicky get-me-out-of-here impulse. All great information. But what is the central point of the sentence? What is its main clause, the bit of information presumably so exciting, so pivotal that every other action in this sentence is mere accessory to it? It's *John realized he was tired.*

We'll talk about clauses in chapter 3. Subsequent chapters will look at some of the other structural issues in this passage. But I wrote this deliberately bad sentence to illustrate an issue we should cover right away—one of the least known but perhaps most helpful concepts for writing good sentences: subordinating conjunctions.

The job of a subordinating conjunction is (drum roll, please) to subordinate. It relegates a clause to a lower grammatical status in the sentence. Subordination is not a bad thing. On the contrary, subordination through the use of conjunctions like *after* is a crucial and interesting dynamic of the language. But when you don't fully understand the power of subordinating conjunctions, they can suck the life out of your writing faster than you can say "rejection letter." The problem they can create is sometimes called upside-down subordination. It's a simple concept. It means that a sentence inadvertently takes some less interesting piece of information like *John was tired* and treats it as though it were more notable than *John shot his business partner in the face*. Occasionally, that might be exactly what the writer intended. But often it's accidental and undermines the sentence.

I first noticed this subordination problem when I started hanging out at writers' Internet message boards. On these sites, aspiring authors often post their query letters—the pitches that authors write to literary agents to try to persuade them to read their manuscripts. The query writers ask others to critique the letters. Many of the letters contain rambling sentences, incoherent sentences, sentences that don't jibe with previous sentences, danglers, comma splices—you name it. But the most troubling mistake occurs when a writer subordinates the interesting action. That is, she relegates the exciting stuff to a lower grammatical status.

Query letters are prone to subordination problems. In a query, an author must synopsize and sell her own book. It is a task that can trip up even the most skilled writer. After all, if an author has just spent a year or two steeped in every minuscule detail of the characters she made up from scratch, it can be hard to see the forest for the trees. She's spent countless hours laboring over the minutiae of her own story, so she can't bring herself to omit the details that just aren't important enough to go in a query. Instead, the writer's solution is to cram in as many exciting details as possible. All too often, the result is a sentence like the one at the beginning of this chapter.

To understand what's wrong with such sentences and to learn to write better ones, you need to take a moment to learn about conjunctions.

Conjunctions, as those of you of a certain age will remember from *Schoolhouse Rock*, are for "hooking up words and phrases and clauses." They're little words like *and*, *if*, *but*, *so*, and *because*. We use them every day with no problem. We seldom stop to think about them.

Conjunctions come in different varieties. The best-known ones— the conjunctions highlighted by *Schoolhouse Rock*—are the coordinators, which are distinct from the subordinators. Coordinators are a small group that includes *and*, *or*, and *but*. Their job is to link units of equal grammatical status:

> I eat oranges and I eat apples.

Here, the coordinator *and* is linking clauses that could stand on their own as sentences: *I eat oranges. I eat apples.* These units are equals. Neither is dependent on the other. They both have something

to say, and their grammar makes clear that they're equally important. *But* and *or* can also be understood this way:

> I eat oranges but I don't eat apples.
>
> I eat oranges but I also eat apples.
>
> I eat oranges but I devour tangerines.
>
> I eat oranges or I eat apples.
>
> I eat oranges or I eat nothing at all.

In each sentence, you have two clauses with the same grammatical
weight, which shows the Reader that they carry the same importance.
Obviously, coordinating conjunctions can link other things besides
whole clauses: *He met Sam and Mickey and Beulah. You can have pizza
or spaghetti or ravioli.* Still, our conjunctions are linking units of the
same grammatical status. In these examples, they're all nouns.

A lot of experts say that the best way to remember all the
coordinating conjunctions is with the acronym FANBOYS, which
represents *for, and, nor, but, or, yet,* and *so.* Others say this is an
oversimplification—that these words don't all work alike. But for our
purposes, this acronym is useful because, by labeling these words as
coordinating conjunctions, we can now set them all aside and begin
talking about subordinating conjunctions.

Subordinating conjunctions are a much larger set. They include
*after, although, as, because, before, if, since, than, though, unless, until,
when,* and *while.*

A lot of common phrases serve as subordinating conjunctions as well. They include *as long as, as though, even if, even though, in order that*, and *whether or not*.

These subordinators all have one thing in common: They subordinate. They relegate information to less critical status. They tell the Reader, "This is just minor info we have to get out of the way before we get to the really big news" or "We're tacking this on as an afterthought to really big news."

Consider this sentence:

Before robbing a bank, Mike was an accountant.

Read it aloud. Notice how, instinctively, your voice wants to rush through all the stuff before the comma, then emphasize the stuff after the comma? That's because our subordinating conjunction, *before*, tells you that what follows is not the main point. The main point will come later, perhaps after a deep breath or a pause.

There's nothing wrong with putting the main point last. A main clause can come at the beginning, middle, or end of a sentence. But it's usually a bad idea to beat down that information by subordinating it.

Ninety-nine out of a hundred people would agree that robbing a bank is more interesting than working as an accountant. There may be contexts in which this is not true, like in a study examining the long-term psychological effects of accounting work. But usually bank robbery is more notable to Readers than adding up columns of numbers.

In *Before robbing a bank, Mike was an accountant*, we are snuffing the action out of our sentence. We've made the main point *Mike was an accountant*.

But in *After working for twenty-five years as an accountant, Mike robbed a bank*, the main action is robbing. Chances are that's a better choice.

By saying that subordinators relegate information to a lower status, I don't just mean by nuance or tone. It's not just because you read these phrases in a rushed voice. It's more concrete than that. Subordinating conjunctions relegate clauses to lower grammatical status. Which brings us to my favorite grammar magic trick. Look at this sentence:

> Bob likes mustard.

It's a complete sentence—subject, verb, and all. So can you render this complete sentence an incomplete sentence not by taking any words away but by *adding* a word? Yep. If that word is a subordinating conjunction:

> Because Bob likes mustard . . .
>
> If Bob likes mustard . . .
>
> Although Bob likes mustard . . .
>
> As Bob likes mustard . . .
>
> When Bob likes mustard . . .
>
> Unless Bob likes mustard . . .

Ta-da! Our once complete sentence is now less than complete through a process of addition. More is less. Pretty neat, huh? (Don't feel bad if you don't find that as thrilling as I do.) Subordinating conjunctions relegate clauses to a lower *grammatical* status.

Subordination means that what was a whole sentence is whole no more. It's a mere subordinate clause. This is why subordinate clauses are often called dependent clauses: they depend on another clause to make the sentence complete.

Your Reader instinctively knows that a subordinate clause is less important than the main clause that's sure to come up somewhere in your sentence:

> The company resumed regular operations after its president
> failed to acquire a competing firm.

We have two actions in this sentence: a resuming of operations and a failed attempt to acquire a company. One is a big event. The other is a return to business as usual.

Remember that little rant about thy Reader, thy god? That's your guiding light here: what does your Reader most want to know?

There are times when the structure just presented is the best choice. For example, if you already mentioned in a previous sentence the failed acquisition, the example sentence would work fine. There's no need to pound the point home again. Similarly, if your Reader is a shareholder, it's possible that the resumption of regular operations is the most important thing to him. In that case you'd be wise to emphasize the business-as-usual stuff over the failed acquisition. On the other hand, if the failed acquisition is most notable to the reader, take that out of the subordinate clause:

> The company's president failed to acquire a competing firm.
> After the deal fell through, the company resumed regular
> operations.

Again, this illustrates that subordination is not a bad thing. It's a tool. It only becomes a bad thing when you subordinate the stuff most interesting to your Reader while elevating less important information.

Let's look at another example:

> Until Jane can slay the dragon, retrieve the jewel from its belly, and bribe the evil King Goombah, her mission of protecting her townsfolk will remain unfulfilled.

Here, our subordinating conjunction is *until*. And just look at all the stuff it's subordinating: dragon slaying, open-worm surgery, bribing of regents. Pretty interesting stuff to a certain type of Reader. Now look at the main clause: *her mission will remain*. It has a vague subject and weak action.

A sentence like this might be okay after you've already discussed the slaying, jewel-getting, and bribing business. But unless you've already fleshed out these details for your Reader, you're throwing a wet blanket on some interesting action.

Once you're aware of the power of subordination, a whole world of options opens up to you:

> Jane must slay the dragon. Then she must cut the fabled jewel out of its belly and deliver it to the evil King Goombah. It's the only way she can stop the massacre of her townsfolk.

Now that you're getting the hang of this, here's a more subtle example:

> If I'm going to give you ten million dollars, you must use it wisely.

This is not a bad sentence. *If* clauses set up conditions, which can be crucial to your meaning. But because our *if* clause contains the most interesting stuff—a ten-million-dollar gift—it's worth considering whether we can play up that information:

> I'm going to give you ten million dollars if and only if you'll use it wisely.
>
> I'm going to give you ten million dollars on the condition that you use it wisely.
>
> I'm going to give you ten million dollars. Use it wisely.
>
> Here's ten million bucks. Blow it all at the roulette wheel and I'll smack you upside the head.

Some of these alternatives might fit the bill for your Reader. Some might not. Some might remain true to the facts. Some might not. As you can see, every rewrite contains the danger that you'll lose or warp important information. For example, our third and fourth alternatives take out the *if* and thus remove all signs of conditionality. In the last example, which begins *Here's ten million bucks*, the speaker clearly doesn't want the listener to squander the money. But she's giving it to him either way. What's iffy now is not whether he'll get the money but whether he'll spend it in a way that gets him that smack upside the head.

The Reader's needs should dictate which information you subordinate. If you subordinate the information about a ten-million-dollar gift, it should be a choice—a result of the power you wield over words.

A skilled writer can use upside-down subordination as a device to make things astoundingly right-side-up. The best example I've seen is pointed out in Francine Prose's *Reading Like a Writer*. It is a passage from Tim O'Brien's *The Things They Carried*—a passage seemingly dedicated to the mundane possessions like canned peaches and pocketknives that some soldiers hauled on their backs through a jungle during wartime. In the middle of this listlike passage appears the sentence "Ted Lavender, who was scared, carried tranquilizers until he was shot in the head outside the village of Than Ke in mid-April." Then, after seven sentences of information like how much the soldiers' helmets weighed and the material that lined their ponchos, O'Brien tosses in, "In April, for instance, when Ted Lavender was shot, they used his poncho to wrap him up, then carry him across the paddy, then lift him into the chopper that took him away."

Lavender's death is subordinated. Twice. On purpose and to great effect. The writer was grammatically downplaying a soldier's being shot dead in order to create a chilling commentary on the significance of one life in wartime and the speed with which it can end. It's a feat that wasn't lost on Prose herself. She notes O'Brien's skill at illustrating "the possibility of being shot, like Ted Lavender, suddenly and out of nowhere: not only in the middle of a sentence but in the midst of a subordinate clause."

Does that inspire you to master the concept of subordination and subordinating conjunctions? I hope so, because we have more work to do. Let's look at some more ways that poorly chosen subordinators can hurt your writing. For example, one subordinating conjunction that seems to sabotage a lot of fiction is *as*:

> A bewildered look came over Cyrus's face as the sword
> pierced his armor and he fell to the ground.

There are two problems with the use of *as* here. First, it's subordinating the action. Someone just skewered Cyrus. Yet the writer did not see fit to make that the main clause. As with all subordination matters, there's room to debate whether this was a bad choice. I believe it was. But there's another problem with our *as* that's clearly worse.

As suggests simultaneous action. You brush your teeth *as* you read the paper. This is one of several definitions of the word. So our sentence seems to say that Cyrus was getting stabbed, making a face, and falling all at the same moment. My knowledge of sword fights may be based on nothing more than a Brad Pitt movie, but I'm pretty sure those things would happen in sequence and not all at once.

As you can see, upside-down subordination is not the only danger presented by subordinating conjunctions. Some carry added danger in their definitions. The quintessential example is *while*:

> While walking through the park is good exercise, jogging is
> better.

Some people will tell you this is an out-and-out misuse of *while*. They say that *while* can refer only to a time span and can never be used to mean *although*. *Webster's New World College Dictionary* begs to differ. *While* can indeed be a synonym for *although*. But it's often a very, very bad one. If the spirit strikes you, vow to use *while* only by its main definition: "during or throughout the time that."

While walking through the park seems to be setting up something that happened during that walk: *While walking through the park,*

Susie saw a squirrel. But midway through our sentence it becomes clear that this is not the meaning of *while* that the writer intended. The writer could have saved the Reader this potential confusion simply by choosing the more accurate *although*:

> Although walking through the park is good exercise,
> jogging is better.

Of course, not all uses of *while* for *although* are as confusing:

> While it is always a good idea to bring an umbrella,
> today will likely be sunny.

If that sentence came across my desk for copyediting, I'd leave the *while* intact.

Another subordinator that poses its own unique dangers is *if*:

> If you enjoy seafood, the restaurant offers many fresh
> fish selections.

This is another example of a subordinating conjunction making mischief not through subordination but through logic. You see, the restaurant manager doesn't call you to ask if you enjoy seafood before he decides on the menu. His restaurant offers fresh fish whether you like it or not. But our sentence doesn't accurately reflect this. Our sentence says the menu offerings are contingent on your preferences. The writer meant

> For those who enjoy seafood, the restaurant offers many
> fresh fish selections.

or

If you enjoy seafood, note that the restaurant offers many
fresh fish selections.

or

If you enjoy seafood, you'll be happy that the restaurant offers
many fresh fish selections.

In some cases, illogical uses of *if* are so common that they're
pretty much acceptable:

If you want me, I'll be in my room.

Everyone knows what this speaker means. Yes, it's true that she'll
be in her room regardless of whether the listener wants her. But I
have no problem with that. It's a common expression that's clearly
understood. Use your own judgment in such cases. Just be aware
that more complex and less familiar *if* constructions can create big
problems.

Since is a controversial subordinating conjunction. Some people
say it can't be used as a synonym for *because*. They say that *since* refers
to a time span and *because* refers to cause-and-effect relationships. In
fact, dictionaries allow *since* as a synonym for *because*. So use it that
way if you like, but use it well.

Since is like *while* in that its time-related definition has the power
to confuse:

Since you've graduated from Harvard, can you tell me how the
professors are?

Here the subordinate clause sounds at first like it's referring to
a time period, as it would in, *Since you've graduated from Harvard,*

you've gotten a lot of job offers. You have to get halfway through the sentence to know that the writer was using the "because" meaning of *since*.

Than is another booby-trapped conjunction:

> Do you like Coldplay more than Madonna? If so, how do you
> know? Have you asked her?

It's common to drop a verb after *than*. We do that because the verb that would come after *than* is the same as a verb that appeared somewhere before: *Joe is taller than Sue* is a shortened way of saying *Joe is taller than Sue is. Bernice runs faster than Stanley* means *Bernice runs faster than Stanley runs.* But be careful. Your Reader may need a little more help than that.

Do you like Coldplay more than Madonna? leaves implied a second occurrence of the verb *like*, but we don't know who's doing the liking. You could mean *Do you like Coldplay more than you like Madonna?* or *Do you like Coldplay more than Madonna likes Coldplay?* There's no rule here other than to remember the pitfalls and be careful.

If you find all this a little overwhelming, don't worry. Though it may take a while to get comfortable with these concepts, you need not immediately commit to memory every subordinating conjunction and its potential hazards. Your goal is to start to recognize subordinating conjunctions in your writing and in your reading—to see the power they afford you to serve your Reader. These words help you organize your thoughts, say what you mean, emphasize what's most important, and even create art. If that takes a while, it's time well spent.

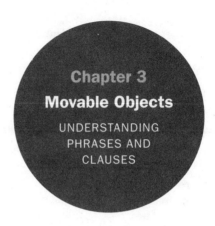

Chapter 3

Movable Objects

UNDERSTANDING PHRASES AND CLAUSES

A clause is a unit that usually contains a subject and a verb.

A phrase is a unit of one or more words that works as either a noun, a verb, an adverb, an adjective, or something called a prepositional phrase.

Sorry to jump straight into hard-core grammar talk without buying you dinner first. But this really is great stuff for a writer to know. With a firm grasp of phrase and clause structure, you'll start to see sentences almost like Lego sculptures made up of modular, movable, interlocking pieces. This will do great things for your writing. I promise. We saw some of the potential in the last chapter. But the only way to get there is by hunkering down with some serious grammar. As Stephen King wrote, "Grammar is not just a pain in the ass; it's the pole you grab to get your thoughts up on their feet and walking." So stay with me through the academic part, and I'll make it as quick as possible and well worth your while.

Start by noting that a clause, because it contains a subject and a verb, can make up a whole sentence: *Jesse dances. Jesse danced. Jesse has danced.* Or a clause can be just part of a larger sentence: *Jesse has danced the tango with a happily married septuagenarian woman who was wearing Spanx.* A phrase, however, cannot stand on its own as a complete sentence. A phrase is a single word or a cluster of words that together work in your sentence as a single part of speech. As we have seen, phrases come in five varieties: noun phrases, verb phrases, adverb phrases, adjective phrases, and prepositional phrases. To get a better understanding of phrases, let's analyze that last Jesse sentence:

> Jesse has danced the tango with a happily married septua-
> genarian woman who was wearing Spanx.

Jesse is a noun phrase. I know it's odd to think of a single word as a phrase. Indeed, that's a little out of sync with the everyday definition. But the *Oxford English Grammar* includes one-word units as phrases, and for our purposes this works best. Phrases can have phrases within them. So just know that *Jesse, Jesse Wilson, Big Bad Jesse, the man called Jesse,* and *Jesse of Sunnybrook Farm* are all noun phrases. Any of them might function as a noun in a sentence. That's what we're concerned with here: their job in a sentence. Every phrase has a headword—the word on which any other words are hinged. So in *Jesse of Sunnybrook Farm, Jesse* is the headword, and because it's a noun, this is a noun phrase.

Has danced is a verb phrase. It contains the auxiliary *has* and the past participle *danced.* Together, they convey the action and when it occurred. They're working as a unit to perform a single job in the sentence.

The tango is another noun phrase. In our sentence, it's the object of the verb, unlike our other noun phrase, *Jesse*, which is the subject of the verb. Subjects perform the action in a verb. Objects receive the action—they're the things being acted upon. Nouns can do either job. So just see that *Jesse* and *the tango* are both nouns—*things*—in this sentence. They both qualify as noun phrases.

With is a preposition. We'll talk more about prepositions in chapter 9. But for now, remember that these include words like *with, of, to, at, in, above, before,* and so on. It's crucial to note that a preposition takes an object—usually a noun phrase. The preposition and its object are a team. Therefore, our preposition *with* has the object *a happily married septuagenarian woman*. Together, they're our prepositional phrase. Note that the object of a preposition could also be a pronoun: *with her.*

As we saw earlier, verbs also can take objects. In fact, verbs and prepositions are the only two parts of speech that do this. But not all verbs do. The ones that do are called transitive. So in *I see Betty* the word *Betty* is the object of the verb *see.* In *I dance with Betty* the word *Betty* is the object of the preposition *with.* Both uses of *Betty* can be swapped out for a pronoun: *I see **her*** and *I dance with **her.*** Remember that and you'll be far ahead of most people in understanding objects—not to mention prepositional phrases.

Happily is an adverb phrase. But wait a minute, you say. Didn't we already account for *happily* as part of our prepositional phrase? Yep, we did. However, phrases can be contained within phrases within phrases. So our prepositional phrase *with a happily married septuagenarian woman* contains other phrases, including the adverb phrase *happily*, which is modifying the adjective *married.*

31

Happily married is an adjective phrase. It contains our adverb and our adjective, and together they work as a unit to modify the noun *woman*. The noun phrase *happily married woman* contains the adjective phrase *happily married*, which contains the adjective phrase *married* and the adverb phrase *happily*. They're all modifying *woman*. Dizzy? Don't worry. Just remember that phrases can work like nesting dolls and you'll be okay.

Septuagenarian is also an adjective phrase. In some cases this word would be a noun—*A septuagenarian stole my bike*—but here it's modifying the noun *woman*, so it's working as an adjective.

Woman is a noun phrase.

Who was wearing Spanx is a relative clause. It's a modifier, which means it works like an adjective, adding extra description to the noun that comes before it: *woman*.

If you find this stuff difficult, that's okay. It is difficult. You don't need to have it all down now. You just need to begin to identify phrases and clauses in your reading and writing. Start looking for them, especially prepositional phrases, which can be the most helpful to a writer and also the most fun, as we'll see in chapter 9. Until then, suffice it to say that prepositional phrases are the key to fully enjoying the supposedly real classified advertisement that once offered for sale "mixing bowl set designed to please cook with round bottom for efficient beating"!

As for clauses, you already have a good foundation for understanding them from our chapter on subordination. So, remembering that a clause usually contains a noun and a verb—a doer of an action and the action itself—can you identify all the clauses in the following sentence?

> After Floyd spoke, Lou laughed.

What are the two actions here? There's some speaking going on and there's some laughing going on. Do we have doers of those actions? Yes, Floyd and Lou are the people doing those things. Each is paired up with an action in a way that makes Floyd and Lou subjects of verbs in this sentence. So now that you know what's being done and who's doing it, you can identify the two basic clauses: *Floyd spoke* and *Lou laughed*.

At this point, you can also identify the main clause of the sentence. Thinking back to our chapter on subordinators, remember that *after* is often a subordinating conjunction and, like all subordinating conjunctions, makes a previously independent clause suddenly unable to stand on its own as a sentence:

> Floyd spoke. [complete sentence]

> After Floyd spoke . . . [subordinate clause that does not qualify as a complete sentence]

True, in casual speech and writing, people use fragments as complete sentences all the time. That's why you commonly see stuff like *When did I leave? After Floyd spoke.* That's fine. But even then, *After Floyd spoke* is a fragment and not a complete sentence.

Instead of subordinating one of our clauses, we could, if we wanted to, coordinate them:

> Floyd spoke and Lou laughed.

The coordinating conjunction *and* is linking two equally weighted clauses. In fact, these two are so equally weighted that you could swap their order: *Lou laughed and Floyd spoke, Floyd spoke and Lou laughed*—it's all good. Sure, the meaning is different from our first example, in which Lou laughed only *after* Floyd spoke. But that's precisely why sometimes you want to subordinate—for the extra meaning you can convey:

Although Floyd spoke, Lou laughed.

Because Floyd spoke, Lou laughed.

When Floyd spoke, Lou laughed.

While Floyd spoke, Lou laughed.

Until Floyd spoke, Lou laughed.

Although Lou laughed, Floyd spoke.

Because Lou laughed, Floyd spoke.

Floyd spoke. Lou laughed.

These demonstrate some of the ways that clauses can be moved around, combined with conjunctions, and made to convey your exact meaning.

A few more things you should know about clauses before we move on: Not all have two words or even a subject. Most commands, for example, contain only an implied subject. *Stop!* is a complete clause and even a complete sentence because, in English, commands—called imperatives—drop the subject, which is *you*:

[You] Stop!

[You] Go away!

[You] Run like the wind!

[You] Listen!

Also, in a sentence like *Joe wanted to cry*, the infinitive verb *to cry* is considered a clause—called a nonfinite clause because it's not conjugated in a way that shows time. In *Joe doesn't like crying*, the word *crying* is also considered a nonfinite clause. Don't worry. These are not need-to-know facts for crafting great sentences. But there's an irony here that shouldn't be overlooked: clauses are defined as units that usually contain a subject and a verb, but they don't always fit their own definition. Still, if you think of clauses in these simplest terms and just remember that there are exceptions, you'll do fine.

Phrases are even more portable than clauses and their placement is even more likely to affect your meaning. We'll see more examples of the power of both these units throughout the rest of this book. For now, begin to think of phrases and clauses as the basic parts of every sentence. Start to identify them. Start to see other ways phrases and clauses could work within the same sentence. And pat yourself on the back for getting through this chapter.

Now let's move on to something fun.

Chapter 4

Size Matters

SHORT VERSUS LONG
SENTENCES

Here's a great opening sentence for a magazine article:

> Alec Baldwin has the unbending, straight-armed gait of some-
> one trying to prevent clothes from rubbing against sunburned
> skin.

This sentence is not just interesting and visual, it's very effective at setting the tone for the article. You can tell right away that the writer has a unique take on Baldwin. With just one sentence, the writer has evoked that riveted sensation you get when you can't look away from a four-car pileup on the side of the freeway. It's clear that this will not be the typical fawning feature article. It will not read as though it were pitched by Baldwin's publicist. There's no doubt you're in for a good read.

But what if the writer, in the middle of this sentence, decided that there were some other bits of information that just couldn't wait till sentence two? What if she said, "Ah, crud. I had a good sentence here but if I don't squeeze in something about Baldwin's work and state of mind, I may never get another opportunity"?

You might end up with something like this:

> Alec Baldwin, who stars in *30 Rock*, the NBC sitcom that has revived his career and done nothing to lift his spirits, has the unbending, straight-armed gait of someone trying to prevent clothes from rubbing against sunburned skin.

This is a textbook example of how longer sentences can sabotage writing. The inserted information is an interruption. When you look at the grammar, you see it's a clunky interruption at that. The writer has inserted a relative clause, *who stars in 30 Rock*, which is then restated as an appositive, *the NBC sitcom*, which in turn is modified by not just another relative clause but a double-duty relative clause: *that has revived his career and done nothing to lift his spirits*. We'll talk about those terms later. But for now the important thing is that all this bulky stuff comes between the subject and the main verb, *has*. You have to trudge through all that stuff just to get to the main point. Pretty much any freshman English teacher or *Palookaville Post* copy editor will tell you this is the wrong call.

There's just one problem. The longer version of the Alec Baldwin sentence, not the shorter one, was the opening sentence of an article in one of the most respected magazines in the country: the *New Yorker*.

A lot of people will tell you that the longer sentence is always the lesser sentence. Some even say long sentences are an out-and-out no-no. But it's not that simple.

Personally, I have a strong bias in favor of short sentences. I suspect that the *New Yorker*'s not-infrequent use of longer, clunkier forms is a deliberate flouting of conventional wisdom—a sort of "We don't take orders from freshman comp teachers because we're the *New Yorker*, dammit" approach. But I could be wrong. Plenty of people in the world would prefer the longer sentence. The writer and/or editors of the *New Yorker* may be among them.

In fact, you could argue that the second sentence carries some unique benefits. It shakes up the Reader by defying conventional form. As such, it has an ability to command attention that the shorter version does not. Further, some of the inserted stuff actually bolsters the point of the sentence. In particular, the fact that Baldwin's successful show has *done nothing to lift his spirits* is both relevant and juicy. It gives further insight into why this guy might walk around as though he's trying not to rub a sunburn. And though we could find plenty wrong with the real *New Yorker* sentence, it's actually quite skillful and effective.

Now compare two more long sentences:

> After being rebuffed as the next head football coach at Boston College after Jeff Jagodzinski was fired two weeks ago and after not being hired at the University of Massachusetts after Don Brown left to become the defensive coordinator at the University of Maryland, Boston College assistant head coach and offensive line coach Jack Bicknell Jr. is moving to the NFL, as an assistant offensive line coach of the New York Giants, according to several sources close to the program.

and

> The play—for which Briony had designed the posters, programs and tickets, constructed the sales booth out of a

folding screen tipped on its side, and lined the collection box in red crêpe paper—was written by her in a two-day tempest of composition, causing her to miss a breakfast and a lunch.

The first one—the opening sentence of a *Boston Globe* sportswriter's blog—reads as though the writer couldn't wrap his head around the sequence of events. The second sentence reads as though the writer had an intimate knowledge of a complex series of events and all the sights and smells and sounds and emotions attached to them. So you won't be surprised to learn that the second one is the opening sentence of Ian McEwan's prizewinning novel *Atonement*.

Though it's leaps and bounds better than the sportswriter's sentence, I'm not a big fan of McEwan's sentence. To me, it's unnecessarily busy. I don't like the passive *was written by her*. I don't like the stiff and awkward *for which Briony* or how it sort of turns the sentence upside down. And the copy editor in me is almost offended by McEwan's choice to squeeze a whopping thirty-two words between the subject and the verb. But if I were the copy editor, I wouldn't change a word. I can't see any way to restructure it that doesn't take away from the author's voice and his style and the effect he's working to create—elements that should never be discounted or sanitized into oblivion to accommodate sentence-length sticklers or by-the-book copy editors. It seems that the very things I don't like about the sentence are things McEwan was trying to convey: the sentence is *tempest*-like. If he was trying to create a sense of frenetic passion-driven activity, mission accomplished. It's not my cup of tea. I'm more a fan of Kurt Vonnegut's one-word paragraph, "Listen." But that's just me.

Compare two more examples and you'll see why, in general, I'm biased toward shorter sentences:

> I killed him even though I didn't want to because he gave me no choice.

> I killed him. I didn't want to. He gave me no choice.

I believe that modern sensibilities are more attuned to short sentences. Media culture is partly responsible. Think about it. We spend countless hours listening to thirty-second TV commercials that contain six, eight, ten sentences each. But we know that most of the words are just filler. Each commercial has only one central message that boils down into one sentence: "Windex doesn't leave streaks." "Drive a Mustang and you'll be popular with the ladies." "If you really love your kids, you'll buy Purell hand sanitizer." The central message is supplemented with extra sentences used to hammer home the same point. As a culture, we're becoming ever more inclined to tune out fluff. Stripped-down-bare information is an anomaly that can command our attention and our respect.

Another problem with our longer sentence: extra words can have a diluting effect. In *I killed him even though I didn't want to because he gave me no choice*, the linking terms *even though* and *because* seem mealymouthed. It's like the writer is scrambling to explain herself, speaking from a weak, pleading position. It's almost ironic how the facts stand stronger when they stand alone, unmitigated by the writer's urge to overexplain: *I killed him. I didn't want to. He gave me no choice.*

Still, anyone who tells you straight out that short sentences are superior is either overlooking or discounting some of the most respected writers of all time.

So, then, what's the verdict? Are short sentences better or not?

Allow me to end this debate once and for all. Here's how you should look at it: Brevity is a tool. It's a very powerful tool. You don't have to use it. But you have to know how. If you're going to use long sentences, it should be by choice, not due to bumbling ineptitude. Every long sentence can be broken up into shorter ones, and if you don't know how—if you don't see within your long sentences groupings of simple, clear ideas—it will show.

You should master the art of the short sentence, even if you prefer longer ones. All you have to do is start looking at every sentence as a group of phrases and clauses. See in each sentence how every bit of information could carry a sentence of its own. Then you'll have the power to decide exactly how to organize your information.

Let's practice:

> Job hunters read and hear all the time that it's not always enough simply to be qualified for a job because, if other qualified candidates are pursuing and competing for the same vacancy, how well you distinguish yourself from the competition is also critical to getting hired.

This sentence did not appear in print. It's the result of my playing Dr. Frankenstein with another writer's words, which I have disguised. (You're welcome, other writer.) But trust me when I tell you that the original wasn't much better.

Now let's look at the clauses in this sentence:

> job hunters read
>
> and [job hunters] hear
>
> it's [not always enough]

Remember that *it's* means *it* and *is*, which together form a whole clause.

> to be [qualified]

Remember we said that infinitives can also be categorized as clauses.

> other qualified candidates are pursuing
>
> and [other qualified candidates are] competing
>
> you distinguish
>
> [this distinguishing] is [critical]
>
> to getting [hired]

The last one is another nonfinite clause.

As you can see, clauses are not all ideas unto themselves. They can do different jobs in a sentence. For example, *how you distinguish yourself* has at its heart the clause *you distinguish*. But it's not an action in our sentence. It's working with the *how* to function as a subject of a verb: *How you distinguish yourself is critical*. The main verb of this sentence is *is*. The subject is the whole *how* clause. Here are some other examples of how a clause can work like a noun to serve as a subject: *What I want is a soda. How you look is important. Whatever you do is okay with me. That you love me is all I need to know.* In all these sentences, the main verb is *is*, and in all these sentences, the subject—the doer of the action—is a whole clause.

Now let's separate some of the bits of information in this sentence. For this breakdown, we're not looking for clauses but for all the individual ideas in the sentence:

- There is something that job hunters frequently hear.
- It is also something they frequently read.
- Being qualified for a job isn't always enough to land a job.
- Other candidates may be pursuing the same vacancy.
- Other candidates may be competing for the same vacancy.
- Distinguishing yourself is critical to getting hired.

Do you see unnecessary information in here? Is it really important to note that job hunters hear *and* read this? Why stop there? Why not say they hear and read and sniff out and deduce and realize and innately understand and feel with their fingertips while reading Braille and any other activity that conveys information to your brain? No doubt, the writer believed she'd be remiss if she overlooked the fact that job seekers both read and hear it. My advice: Be remiss. It's okay to just say, "They hear it all the time," as long as your Reader understands. There's no need to include a laundry list of all the ways that a job seeker might encounter the information.

Another bit of unnecessary information in our sentence is that business about other candidates *pursuing and competing for* the same vacancy. Even more than the *see and read* stuff, this is a major duh. *Pursuing the same vacancy* means competing. Also, how is competing for the *same* job different from *competing for the job*? The word *compete* already suggests that it's the same job. Adding the word *same* creates a redundancy on top of the redundancy *pursuing and competing for*.

So, what would you do with our original Frankensentence? The possibilities are infinite. Here, slightly disguised, is what I did:

> Job hunters hear it all the time: It's not always enough to be qualified for a job. You need to distinguish yourself from the competition.

Here's how it would look as a copyedited version of our original sentence, with strikethroughs marking deletions and underscore showing insertions:

> Job hunters ~~read and~~ hear <u>it</u> all the time ~~that~~: It's not always enough ~~simply~~ to be qualified for a job<u>.</u> ~~because if other qualified candidates are pursuing and competing for the same vacancy, how well~~ You <u>need to</u> distinguish yourself from the competition ~~is also critical to getting hired~~.

We brazenly omitted *read and*.

We changed the object of the verb *hear*. In the original, the thing being heard was a whole relative clause: *that it's not always enough . . .* We replaced this long clause with the simple pronoun *it*, then inserted a colon to tell the Reader that we will promptly explain what *it* is.

We lost all mention of *other qualified candidates* who are *competing for* and *pursuing*. That's all summed up quite nicely by *the competition*.

We deleted the whole clause that began *because if other qualified candidates . . .* The Reader already gets that.

44

We found the action in our *how* clause and made it more meaningful by setting it up in a sentence with the main clause *you need*.

Also, we got rid of the fatty adverb *simply*.

Now let's look at a sentence whose disastrousness is a little more straightforward:

> Because Paul had wanted to get into doing masonry work
> since he was in college, due in part to the fact that, as a
> college student, he had always wished he could work with
> his hands, which gave him a satisfaction he had never known
> before and which he discovered only in his third year of school
> when he took metal shop before eventually taking a masonry
> course at the Home Depot, he finally decided it was time for
> him to take the plunge.

Unlike our last sentence, this one contains no tricky uses of clauses as subjects or self-conscious redundancies. It's all good, clear, straightforward information that, unfortunately, has been shoved into the writer's mental Cuisinart. But it's easy to get a handle on it, and your experience with subordinating conjunctions will make this task even easier.

Let's break up the sentence without worrying about flow or organization of information or logic or voice. Just examine some of the basic ideas within and how they might boil down to their own sentences:

- Paul had wanted to do masonry work since he was in college.
- As a college student, he had always wished he could work with his hands.
- It gave him a satisfaction he had never known before.

- He discovered this only in his third year of school.
- He took metal shop.
- Then he took a masonry course at the Home Depot.
- He finally decided it was time to take the plunge.

This breakdown does not give us our end result. For one thing, the writer had used subordinators such as *before* and *when* to make sense of nonchronological information. When we take out those conjunctions, a confusing series of events becomes downright nonsensical. But now we can see that the writer was trying too hard to cram in background information. Also, by breaking this up, we now have neat and distinct ideas that we can move around like dominoes. We can put them into any order we like. Here's the same information put into more logical order:

- Paul wanted to learn how to do masonry work.
- He had wanted this since he was in college.
- In his third year of college, he had taken metal shop.
- Then he took a masonry class at the Home Depot.
- Working with his hands gave him a satisfaction he had never known before.
- He finally decided it was time to take the plunge.

This still needs work. For example, we haven't said *when* he finally decided it was time to take the plunge. In our original sentence, it was clearer that the *when* was now. We lost that in the rewrite. But now we have our information in a more logical—if not chronological—order. Cause-and-effect relationships have begun to reveal themselves. So we're closer to a finished product. And now we can make further choices as to how we want to structure our information and whether to add or omit facts:

> Working with his hands gave Paul a satisfaction he had never known before. He discovered this passion in college when he took metal shop. As soon as the semester ended, he signed up for a masonry class at the Home Depot. Now, at age fifty-one, he could no longer deny that this was the only work he had ever wanted to do. It was time, he decided, to take the plunge.

Another possibility:

> Since college, Paul had wanted to work with his hands. A metal shop class in his third year inspired him to take a masonry class at the Home Depot. Working with his hands gave him a satisfaction he had never known. Finally, thirty years later, he decided it was time to leave the accounting field and pursue his dream.

By the way, don't feel bad if your sentences come out long and rambling at first. For many people, that's just part of the writing process. I write some major stinkers myself. It doesn't mean you're a bad writer or you lack talent. It just means that your process for writing good sentences involves putting your messy ideas on paper before cleaning them up. I suppose some people organize all their thoughts in their head before putting them on paper. Kudos to them. But it doesn't mean they're necessarily better writers. There's nothing wrong with writing sentences that come out clunky at first, as long as you can reread your own writing and see where revisions could make your sentences better.

Let's analyze another sentence. This one's a little trickier than the last. It's based on a real but unpublished sentence by a professional writer:

> In addition to assisting her with the practical aspects of returning to school (such as writing a successful application essay and obtaining financial aid), Elizabeth, the center's advisor, who was always quick with a smile and a word of encouragement, helped Rona address her feelings of self-doubt, uncertainty, and apprehensiveness.

Start by trying to isolate the main clause. Can you find it? The main action of the sentence is *helped* and the person doing the helping—the subject—is Elizabeth. But the writer isn't exactly helping the Reader by cramming fifteen words between the subject and the verb. Yes, it's perfectly okay to separate a subject and its verb, but only when it works. Here, it just adds too many words into an already busy sentence.

And how about that introductory phrase that begins *In addition to*? That's a whole lot of information to get into a single breath. By the way, this is called an adverbial. We'll talk more about adverbs and adverbials in chapter 7. What matters here is, does all that information really fit in our sentence? No.

What to do, then, about this monstrous sentence? Often, the simplest solution is to just drop all the conjunctions and fillers and parentheses and other connecting devices and make simple sentences out of what's left. That is, isolate the clauses and/or distinct ideas and form them into individual sentences:

> Elizabeth assisted Rona with the practical aspects of return-
> ing to school. She helped Rona write an application essay and
> apply for financial aid. Elizabeth was the center's advisor. She
> was always quick with a smile or a word of encouragement.
> She helped Rona address her feelings of self-doubt, uncer-
> tainty, and apprehensiveness.

Now we can see that the very essence of our bad sentence was actually a cluster of clear, simple ideas that can be expressed clearly and simply. The beauty of boiling it down this way is that now you can make more choices. You can rearrange the facts and choose which ones to emphasize. For example, I'd move up and shorten the part about Elizabeth's job title. You can change verb tenses to contrast the historical with the here-and-now, weighing the pros of choosing *Elizabeth **had** assisted* over the simpler *Elizabeth assisted*. (We'll talk more about these verb tenses in chapter 12.) You can insert other words to show things like causality: ***Because** she was always quick with a smile or a word of encouragement, Elizabeth helped Rona with her feelings of self-doubt, uncertainty, and apprehensiveness.* You can question whether *uncertainty* and *self-doubt* are redundant or whether the word *uncertainty* indeed conveys something distinct from *self-doubt*. You can decide whether some information, especially the stuff that had been in parentheses, should be folded into another sentence in order to downplay it a bit.

Personally, I'd go for a clear, no-frills rewrite like this:

> Elizabeth, the center's advisor, assisted Rona with the
> practical aspects of returning to school. She helped Rona
> write an application essay and apply for financial aid. Always

> quick with a smile or a word of encouragement, Elizabeth also helped Rona address her feelings of self-doubt and apprehensiveness.

There's no single right answer. And again, every rewrite contains the danger of lost meaning or lost information or even the possibility you'll make the sentence factually incorrect. So while reworking for clarity, the writer must always keep a tight rein on accuracy and meaning.

But what if you don't want clarity? What if you want a big mess—a sentence that conveys not a series of simple, distinct ideas, but instead a mood, a vibe, a vague sense of things not unlike mist. Then you could end up with a sentence like this:

> At the hour he'd always choose when the shadows were long and the ancient road was shaped before him in the rose and canted light like a dream of the past where the painted ponies and the riders of that lost nation came down out of the north with their faces chalked and their long hair plaited and each armed for war which was their life and the women and children and women with children at their breasts all of them pledged in blood and redeemable in blood only.

Would that make you a bad writer? Would that make you someone who doesn't grasp the power of short sentences or even complete sentences, which this is not? On the contrary, writing that sentence would make you Cormac McCarthy—a Pulitzer winner and, to some, one of the greatest writers of our time. That would also make you an exception to my personal preference for short sentences. I love that McCarthy sentence. It's almost impossible to defend it out of its context in *All the Pretty Horses*. But in context, I feel that it works. It's a mess, but it's supposed to be a mess. The whole is not the sum of its parts. It's something different—less a collection of events and facts and more a mystical, elusive, faraway sense of tragically beautiful things that were and will never be again.

Placement counts, too. One of my biggest problems with the sentence from *Atonement* is that it's the very first sentence of the book. Had the above excerpt from *All the Pretty Horses* been the first sentence in that book, I would never have read the second. But it wasn't. It came as seasoning in a story already well under way, built on a solid foundation that contained lots of simple and straightforward sentences. That made all the difference.

Why do I get to say so? What gives me the right? True, I'm not the world's leading authority on good versus bad long sentences. I'm someone even more important than that. I'm McCarthy's Reader. I have absolute power to say whether his sentence worked for me. And it did. Just as he gambled it would.

If it helps, divide writing into two categories: craft and art. If you're plying the craft of writing, aim to make many of your sentences short. Note the word *many*. Even the most hard-nosed short-sentence advocate will agree that too many short sentences strung together can be downright droning. Mixing short sentences with long ones can make your writing more rhythmically pleasing and therefore more Reader friendly. Writers of business letters, press releases, nonfiction books, genre novels—anyone who is more interested in content than form—usually fall into this writing-as-craft category in which short sentences are probably a virtue.

If, on the other hand, you're shooting for art, all bets are off. Art and beauty, more so than clarity and expediency, are in the eye of the beholder. If you think you can write an eighty-nine-word sentence that creates for your Reader a better experience than would a ten- or fifteen-word sentence, do. Go nuts. But remember, short sentences can be art, too. Any fan of Hemingway can tell you that. McCarthy himself is proof:

> He squatted and watched it. He could smell the smoke.
> He wet his finger and held it to the wind.

McCarthy uses plenty of short sentences, as this excerpt from *The Road* illustrates. He's even into sentence fragments and uses them to great effect. His range proves my point: only someone who can see ideas in their most pared-down form can begin stringing them together in ways that make an outrageously long sentence work.

If you never plan to write a short sentence in your life—even if your hero is Jonathan Coe, whose 13,995-word novel *The Rotters' Club* is all one sentence—you should master the short sentence. Doing so will give you better mastery of your long ones and will help you discover ever-better ways of arranging words in order to create meaning and beauty.

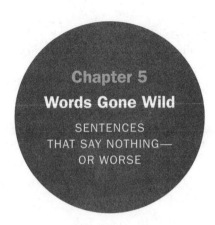

Chapter 5

Words Gone Wild

SENTENCES
THAT SAY NOTHING—
OR WORSE

Hanukkah, celebrated for eight nights, has traditionally meant one gift per night per child. You needn't do the math to figure out the number of gifts and cost when a Jewish grandparent has more than one grandchild.

I love this excerpt. It came across my desk one day while I was copyediting. It's hilarious to me. And sneaky. And insidious. This passage, which was never published and whose author will be glad to remain anonymous, is a classic example of what can happen when a writer stops paying attention to the meaning of her own words. Don't see the problem yet? That's okay. A little less coffee that day and I myself would have missed the delicious absurdity of the statement *You needn't do the math to figure out the number.*

Um, actually, that's what math is.

We can all take a lesson from this: Listen to your words. Choose them carefully. Try to fight the mental palsy that can cause even the best writer to spew nonsense. If you pay attention to your words, you can spot these problems and rewrite in a way that captures what you really mean, perhaps something like this:

> You needn't do the math to see how quickly the costs can mount.

This remains true to what the writer wanted to say. Her point was that these costs compound so quickly that it's immediately evident. This rewrite captures that while eliminating a nonsensical assertion.

Here's another sentence in which the words got away from the writer:

> The concert venue holds higher stakes for its performers by having the reach of a global audience through onsite TV and radio production broadcasting facilities.

This sentence is all-around clunky, but the problem that interests me is *by having the reach of a global audience.* That *of* could be construed to suggest possession. Think, to have the brains *of* Albert Einstein or the wit *of* Stephen Colbert. So, if you have the reach of a global audience, it means that you reach as far as a global audience reaches. But that wasn't the intended meaning. The writer meant that the venue can reach a global audience. The audience is not the reacher but the reachee. Somehow, the writer got too attached to the expression *the reach of* and didn't want to let it go, even after it was clear that it didn't work. All he had to do was think about what he really wanted to say:

> The concert venue holds higher stakes for its performers ~~by having the~~ <u>because it can</u> reach ~~of~~ a global audience through on-site TV and radio production broadcasting facilities.

Here are two more sentences I came across in my copyediting work:

> It's as enticing as the caramel topping on a candied apple.

and

> Autumn is a great time to enjoy the region's ambient weather.

Caramel topping on a candied apple makes me smile. Ambient weather makes me laugh. *Ambient* means "of the surrounding area or environment." Yet the writer seemed to think it was necessary to distinguish that from all the nonambient weather in the region. No doubt, she just liked the sound of her words and didn't think about meaning. I deleted *ambient*.

As for our fusion dessert, if there's some region of the country where people serve those hard-shell, bright red candy apples with a dollop of caramel on top, it still doesn't excuse this sentence. If you find the caramel on an apple enticing, then you probably find a caramel apple enticing. Specifying the part you find most appealing—the topping—isn't worth the extra words. Not in this case, anyway. On the other hand, if the writer loves caramel but doesn't like apples, a caramel apple is not a great example of something that's enticing. Chocolate-covered ants come to mind.

I changed the sentence to

> It's as enticing as a caramel apple.

This problem—the writer paying too little attention to her words—seems most common in news and feature writing. But many novice fiction writers seem to have the opposite problem: They pay too much attention to their words. They try to concoct powerful metaphors. Or they try to find an original turn of phrase. Ironically, they end up having the same problem as the unthinking nonfiction writers: meaning wriggles out of their grasp.

> The sun had stewed all night for that morning. At first light it glared furiously on Lucy's hometown. Lucy was an illness-fated girl. She had passed away during the night. Her body distilled into morning where it slowly began to suppurate. Her basement room drew dark stains as electricity became one with the aged drywall. An indifferent monotone shirred. There was an aroma of singed hair when it happened.

The original version of this disguised excerpt wasn't quite this bad, but it was close, and it contained all the same problems.

When I read stuff like this, I can't help but think of Narcissus. He was the guy from Greek mythology who became so transfixed by his own reflection in a pool of water that he fell in and drowned. If you want to gaze lovingly at your own ability to imagine the sun stewing or a dead body distilling, disconnect your Internet, stick a wad of gum in your flash drive, close the door, and have a ball. Just don't expect your Reader to jump in the reflecting pool with you to willingly drown in the beauty of your words. Metaphors can indeed be beautiful and powerful, but for many writers (present company included) they're very hard to pull off.

I can't tell you how to write good metaphors. But I can offer you a sort of guiding light to help you distinguish good metaphors from bad. You already know it: it's the concept of Reader-serving writing versus writer-serving writing.

A Reader of fiction—be it popular or literary fiction—wants to be told a story. If you can craft metaphors that enhance that story, do. If you can craft metaphors that are so beautiful that they can stand on their own—that they can provide the Reader with as much pleasure as the story—that's an art in itself. But as a rule, if a turn of phrase, a parallel, a comparison, or a metaphor doesn't enhance your Reader's experience, cash it in for straightforward language. That way, though you may not be turning words into divine music of the heart, at least you're not messing up your story.

Here's a bare-bones approach to the same passage that opts for substance over style:

> Lucy had always been a sickly girl. On the night she died, dark stains appeared on the aged drywall of her basement room. The next morning, as the sun beat down mercilessly, there was a mysterious sound—an indifferent monotone. The smell of burned hair hung in the air.

Chances are this would not be well received by the writer. The unpublished author who inspired our passage was in love with his descriptions. Indeed, he openly admitted that he loved the idea of one of his metaphors and didn't want to let it go—even after several other writers told him to bag it.

A lot of Readers might not prefer our revised paragraph, either. (Heck, even I am not totally sold on it.) The rewrite discards a lot of information—facts and imagery some might consider pivotal. But most people would agree that this version better facilitates story. It tells you what happened—not what the sun had been doing during and prior to something happening. And it does so with words whose meanings are clear.

For example, we changed *an indifferent monotone shirred. Monotone* in its original context was painfully unclear. The writer was trying to say that there was a noise coming from somewhere, but *a noise* and *a sound* are far more concrete than *a monotone.* The original raises the question: a monotone *what*? We answered that question by making *monotone* an appositive—a repeat, so to speak—of a new word we brought in: *sound*. When you have a strange sound coming from somewhere unknown, that fact is important and interesting and needs to be treated as such. By stating it outright in clear terms, we do justice to this intriguing story element.

Also, we ditched *shirred*. The writer had misused the word, which really means "to gather up cloth and sew it together in bunches or rows." Even so, this *shirred* almost worked for me—almost. It conjured up something like a whirring, just silkier. But in a passage composed almost exclusively of vague words—words that dance around meaning—some of them had to go. The subject of the original sentence was *a monotone*. The action was *shirred*. A sentence whose core says nothing more than *a monotone shirred* is pure mush that, when surrounded by more mush, just won't do.

We replaced *illness-fated* with *sickly*. Is this because *sickly* is a good word? On the contrary, it's clichéd. But it's still a heck of a lot better than *illness-fated*. Made-up compound modifiers are always risky. You can say a man is doomed to failure, but are you really nailing it when you call him *a failure-doomed man*? Our writer was reaching for a good idea—that Lucy was fated to suffer illnesses. But the writer couldn't find a way to say so in meaningful language. He needed to "kill his darlings"—Stephen King's favorite term for letting go of stuff that just doesn't work.

We ditched the wording about how the walls *drew dark stains*. Did *drew*, a past form of *draw*, mean that the drywall attracted dark stains, the way manure draws flies? Did it mean that the walls sketched the stains, as if with a pen? Neither of these common definitions of *drew* makes sense here. The writer might answer that this ambiguity is exactly what he was shooting for. But that doesn't matter because it doesn't work. So we cashed in *drew dark stains* for plain vanilla language that lets the interesting story detail shine through: *dark stains appeared*.

Of course, these edits are purely subjective. Creative writing need not be bound by things like logic or clarity or common sense. But Reader-serving writing requires that we at least consider such alternatives.

When writing, you may want to call a man "a towering steel-belted radial," you may want to call a woman "a field of lichen," or you may want to call a gun "a glinting and gaping death tube," but before you do, stop and think about whether it's really best for the story and for the Reader.

For quintessential examples of words completely devoid of meaning, you must stray outside both fiction and feature writing to the realm of marketing writing. And if you're looking for the gold standard of empty words, read about spas:

> Customized scrubs and sea salt baths begin with the choice of one of four aroma essences. Each essence, a blend of 100% pure essential oils with certified organic ingredients, is inspired by the elements.

That's right—an essence that's made of essential oils and ingredients! Genius. Of course, it's genius only if you're *trying* to avoid saying anything of substance. But this is a rare situation—rare even for marketing writers because most good marketing writing conveys actual information. Spas are an exception because the only alternative to writing empty words is to say, "We smear mud and food on you for an hour."

The point is: Pay attention to your words. Try not to zone out or become hypnotized by the clichés that live in all our heads and that try to slip into everyone's writing. When you reread your writing, try to do so with a scrutinizing eye that asks, Did I really mean that you don't have to do the math to figure out the number? Is there really any meaning in *a monotone shirred*? Or is there a better way to nail down what I really mean?

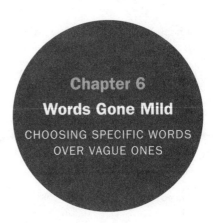

Chapter 6

Words Gone Mild

CHOOSING SPECIFIC WORDS
OVER VAGUE ONES

Which is more compelling?

> The person was moving through the place carrying the things.

or

> The escaped Bellevue patient was hauling ass down the
> diaper aisle grasping a clump of Tom's hair in one hand and
> Grandpa's truss in the other.

Remember this contrast because, though it seems like a no-brainer now, choosing specific words can be harder than you think. In fact, choosing generic, overly broad, noncommittal words is a very common mistake of writers at all levels. Writing, as they say, is about making choices. And the sentence is the tool the fiction writer uses to show her Reader that she is fully committed to the choices she has made. It's the place where the writer of features or news demonstrates that she made an effort to pay attention to details in order to bring the Reader the full experience. Writers do this by choosing the most specific words at their disposal.

Let's look at some of the opaque words that can plague writers and some alternatives to these words.

VAGUE	MORE SPECIFIC	VERY SPECIFIC
Food	Sandwich	Sardine-and-avocado panino au jus
Impact	Benefit	Million-dollar-a-year boost in profits
Proceed	Walk	Meander dreamily
Interact	Flirt	Remove brassiere and shimmy without breaking eye contact
Items	Groceries	Plastic bags spilling over with Lunchables and fabric softener
Effect	Negative side effect	Testicular torsion
Weapon	Firearm	Sawed-off shotgun with a Cindy Lou Who sticker on the oak handle
Noise	Holler	Holler of "Take me, Ronaldo!"
Structure	House	Queen Anne–style McMansion covering 92% of a half-acre lot
Person	Old man	Octogenarian organ-grinder with a handlebar mustache and an ill-tempered monkey

Words like *structure* and *items* and *person* usually have no business in your sentences. They're just wispy shadows of the things they're trying to represent. Ask yourself whether there's a more concrete word that can create a more real experience for your Reader. Sometimes, the answer will be no. But often you'll find that there are much better alternatives to these opaque words.

Whatever you do, don't let laziness or cowardice dictate your word choices. If you're not sure whether your character likes sardines or sleeps with guys named Ronaldo or wears a brassiere, well, sorry. You must figure that out before you pen your final draft because otherwise you're unfairly burdening your Reader: "Geez, I just couldn't decide what kind of gun she would have, so *you* figure it out." The same basic principle applies to journalists and other nonfiction writers. If you didn't notice what the queen was nibbling at as you were interviewing her, you can't just write, "She took a bite of something." Unless you can be more specific, don't mention it at all. You don't have to report every detail, but the details you do report should reflect an effort to create a rich, tactile, immersive experience for the Reader. True, too much description and detail can backfire. But replacing vague words with specific ones is an efficient way to make sentences vivid.

I never want to read that your character heard a noise. I never want to read that the burglar stole some things. I never want to learn that your actions had an effect, that your CEO implemented a new procedure, or that your employees enjoyed a get-together.

I want loud thuds and Omega wristwatches. I want e-mail surveillance and sudden firings. Tell me that your CEO is cracking down on personal phone calls and that the accounting department held its annual drunken square dance and clambake in the warehouse.

Use specific words. Make it a habit to scrutinize your nouns and verbs to always ask yourself whether you're missing an opportunity to create a more vivid experience for your Reader. This habit will open up a world of choices.

> The woman took her car to the dealer to get some needed repairs.

can become

> The retired burlesque dancer drove her rusted pink Lincoln to Smilin' Bob Baxter's GM dealership for a new transmission and new tires and to patch the two dozen cigarette holes in the white leather upholstery.

or

> The decorated veteran of Operation Desert Storm, a recipient of two purple hearts, undid the top button of her Kmart blouse and tried to smile as she drove her sputtering 1984 Celica up to the service window at the glistening Toyota/Lexus dealership.

or

> "Shotgun Granny" Evans squealed her tires as her dusty F-150 pickup truck pulled in to Ward's Ford.

or simply

> Lisbeth drove her Prius to Campbell's Toyota for new brake pads.

Not every sentence needs to be packed with details and descriptors. But learning to pinpoint and root out vague words will give you more choices and therefore more power to construct the best sentence for your piece and for your Reader.

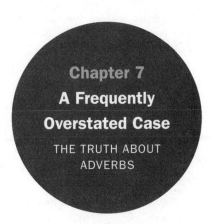

Chapter 7

A Frequently Overstated Case

THE TRUTH ABOUT
ADVERBS

It is, perhaps, the most famous bit of sentence-writing advice of all time: avoid adverbs. Yet I'd guess that about nine out of ten people who spout this advice would flunk the following test. Find all the adverbs in this sentence:

> Knowing well that I can visit you there soon is not really very helpful, as I am not well and therefore cannot prudently travel tomorrow.

Did you catch *prudently*? Good. One point. If you also caught *really*, you're at two points. Did you also catch *well*? Excellent, but only if you counted it once. The second *well* is not an adverb, only the first one is. So, assuming you got all those right, you're at three points. Pat yourself on the back because three out of eight ain't bad.

That's right, there are eight—count 'em, eight—adverbs in this sentence. They are *well* (the first but not the second one), *there, soon, really*, *very*, *therefore*, *prudently*, and *tomorrow*. Yep, this *tomorrow* is an adverb. Don't believe me? Look it up in your dictionary. I'll wait.

When people say that adverbs hurt writing, they're talking about a specific kind of adverb, called a manner adverb—even though they may not realize it. Manner adverbs are the ones that describe the manner in which an action occurred: *walk **quickly**, eat **slowly**, dance **enthusiastically***. When people say to avoid them, there's some wisdom in their advice, but only for those wise enough to understand it. So before we get into what this advice means and when to apply it, let's hunker down and get a basic understanding of adverbs.

Adverbs are the best-kept secret of the grammar world. Their true identity is cleverly hidden in plain view. I consider it one of the great mysteries of our language that, though we all learned about adverbs in school and though many of us can still remember the *Schoolhouse Rock* adverbs song, almost nobody knows what an adverb is.

Here is the best way to understand what an adverb is. Adverbs answer the questions

- when? *I'll see you **tomorrow***.
- where? *Go play **outside***.
- in what manner? *Sue ran **quickly***.
- how much or how often? *You're **very** early. You're **rarely** late.*

Adverbs also give commentary on whole sentences: ***Frankly**, my dear, I don't give a damn.* Those are called sentence adverbs. And they can create a link to the previous sentence: ***Consequently**, the engine exploded.* Those are called conjunctive adverbs.

Adverbs can modify verbs (*Mark whistles **happily***), adjectives (*Betty is **extremely** tall*), other adverbs (*Mark whistles **extremely happily***), or whole sentences (***However**, I don't care*).

But there are also things called adverbials, which may or may not be adverbs:

> *Additionally*, there will be cake.

> *In addition*, there will be cake.

Think of an adverbial as any unit doing an adverb's job: answering *when*, *where*, or *in what manner*, or modifying a whole thought. So in our first example, we have a conjunctive adverb, *additionally*, working as an adverbial. But in our second example, we have a prepositional phrase, *in addition,* working as an adverbial. Think of *adverb* as a word class—a club. *Adverbial* is a job. And often the dictionary makers get the final say on whether any word does the job enough to earn membership in the club. That's why your dictionary probably says that *tomorrow* can be an adverb but that *Tuesday* is exclusively a noun. In *I'll see you **tomorrow***, the word *tomorrow* is an adverb doing the job of an adverbial, answering the question *when*. But in *I'll see you **Tuesday***, the word *Tuesday* is a noun doing the same job. *Tuesday* does not qualify as an adverb only because most dictionary makers haven't admitted it into the club.

A lot of words that are adverbs also count as other parts of speech. For instance, if you look up *tomorrow*, you see that it's also a noun, depending on its job in a sentence. In *Tomorrow can't come soon enough*, the word *tomorrow* performs the action of the verb. So it's a noun. In *I'll see you tomorrow*, the same word answers the question *when*. So it's an adverb.

Well is an adverb when it describes an action. But look it up and you'll see that it's also an adjective meaning "in good health." So the *well* in *I am well* is actually a different word from the *well* in *I do well*.

Full mastery of adverbs takes time and, frankly, isn't necessary for our goal of writing good sentences. But there are three things you should remember about adverbs:

1. Adverbs are a very broad group that includes those *-ly* words we all learned, but also many other types of words. To identify adverbs, think of them as words that answer the questions *when, where, how, to what degree*, and *in what manner*. When in doubt, check a dictionary. Better yet, check two or three.

2. When someone tells a writer to avoid adverbs, the speaker really means avoid manner adverbs—the ones that answer the questions *in what manner* and *to what degree*.

3. Adverbials can be single words or whole phrases that inject when-, where-, or how-type information into your sentence (*I'll exercise **on Monday***) or offer commentary on the whole sentence: ***Tragically**, Jonas was fired. **In consequence**, he found a new job.*

Now, at long last, we can talk about that age-old bit of writing advice: avoid (manner) adverbs. When people tell you to avoid adverbs, they often have in mind sentences like these:

> Brenda Bee is the author of two books on knitting and has previously written three children's books.

> Yuri was formerly a dancer with the Bolshoi ballet for eleven
> years.

The manner adverbs in these examples stink. Period. The adverbs
are redundant. What's the difference between *Bee has written* and *Bee
has previously written*? Nada. Our Yuri sentence, too, uses an adverb
to repeat information already conveyed by a verb: *Was a dancer* has
the same meaning as *was formerly a dancer*. Adding *formerly* creates a
droning "blah-blah-blah" effect that tells the Reader, "Hey, I wasn't
paying attention to my own words, so why should you?"

Let's look at another example:

> People who aren't happy in their jobs may be more likely
> to stay with their current employers than look for new ones
> because they see so many Americans involuntarily losing
> their jobs.

This sentence is from a piece by a professional columnist, which
proves that even the best of us can encounter adverb problems. *Invol-
untarily losing their jobs*, in this sentence at least, is not one iota different from just plain old *losing their jobs*. The Reader gets the message
and doesn't need to be told that getting canned is involuntary.

When we eliminate the adverb, we take out a redundancy. But we
also streamline the sentence for some less-is-more value:

> because they see so many Americans losing their jobs.

This is a sentence-level microcosm of that most iconic bit of writing advice: show, don't tell. Job loss is a thing. The Reader can see
it for what it is. He doesn't need it gussied up with descriptions or
value judgments. You can use an adverb to tell what an action was

like: *Kevin slammed the door forcefully.* But you're better off showing the results of that action: *Kevin slammed the door, shattering the wood.*

Now let's look at another way manner adverbs can go wrong:

> Ralph maniacally gave Joseph a sneer, then crazily and angrily began walking toward him.

> "I want you," Aileen purred sexily.

These sentences illustrate a more subtle problem that is best summed up by a line from the 2007 film *American Gangster.*

In that movie, Frank Lucas, played by Denzel Washington, is a powerful 1970s crime boss who dresses with no more flash than a bank manager. His simple style is in stark contrast to the styles of his pimped-out sable-fur-wearing contemporaries. His reason for this understated image: "The loudest person in the room is the weakest person in the room."

In our examples, the manner adverbs are supposed to make the action more exciting. But in fact, they weaken the action. *Ralph gave Joseph a sneer, then began walking toward him* has an understated oomph that's lost when you try to drum it home with *maniacally, crazily,* and *angrily.* *"I want you," Aileen purred* doesn't need *sexily* to convey sex. Leave something to the imagination. Simplicity and austerity are powerful.

Adverbs can weaken the very ideas they're trying to beef up. Returning to an example we used in chapter 4, compare

> I brutally killed him. I truly didn't want to. But he ultimately gave me absolutely no choice.

to

I killed him. I didn't want to. He gave me no choice.

You can see why I hang with the anti-adverbs people. But adverb defenders have a point, too. Often, manner adverbs achieve the desired effect:

Penny left quickly.

He stared at her longingly.

Clean this mess up immediately.

Senator Snide laughed cruelly.

"I want you to leave," Nora said simply.

Like all words, manner adverbs should be carefully chosen. They should carry some benefit that overrides the less-is-more principle. They should not create redundancies, and they should be free of that weak "look at me" quality to which they're so prone. They should not appear to be telling the stuff that your nouns and verbs should be showing.

Only when you've asked yourself whether your sentence is better off without a manner adverb can you decide whether that adverb deserves to stay.

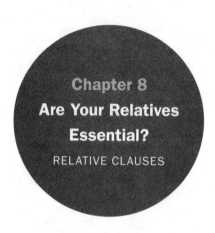

Chapter 8
**Are Your Relatives
Essential?**
RELATIVE CLAUSES

In the last chapter, we saw how adverbs work as modifiers. They're similar to adjectives, which are also modifiers. A lot of people know that. But whole phrases and clauses can also be modifiers. As you'll see in this chapter and the two that follow, understanding phrases and clauses as modifiers is key to mastering the art of the sentence. We'll start with the easiest of these topics, relative clauses, before moving on to prepositional phrases in chapter 9 and participial phrases in chapter 10.

Let's look at how one successful pro uses relative clauses:

> Wednesday had traded the Lincoln Town Car, which Shadow had liked to drive, for a lumbering and ancient Winnebago, which smelled pervasively and unmistakably of male cat, which he didn't enjoy driving at all.

I love this passage from Neil Gaiman's *American Gods* because it's another example of how a writing no-no can be a total yes-yes in the right hands. The no-no in play is the stacking of one relative clause on top of another, which could result in something like this:

> The house that Joe was living in, which had a furnace that burned only coal, which was becoming scarce in Virginia, which was ground zero for the nation's coal shortage, which was the result of a policy by the new president, who opposed coal mining and burning, which were causing too much pollution, which was choking the planet that desperately needed CO_2 reduction . . .

See how this can go on forever like some kind of cosmic nesting doll? With each added relative clause, we get further and further away from our main point, further down the rabbit hole of minutiae and minutiae about minutiae. We were talking about one character's house. But we got way off track. As such, overuse of relative clauses is disorienting at best and rude at worst. It's like telling the Reader, "We're talking about Joe's house and you need to remember that for a long time even as I mention lots of other things because, when I'm done, I'm not going to tell you again that we're talking about Joe's house. It's your job to remember." See what I mean by rude?

But Gaiman pulled off the feat of stacking his relative clauses. He used them to create a rhythm. He managed to underscore—almost musically—a fun irony: Shadow's nice Town Car had been replaced by a beat-up Winnebago that, adding insult to injury, reeked of cat spray. That's skillful writing. And skill is bred of understanding, or at the very least of practice. So let's take a minute to understand relative clauses and the words that make them: relative pronouns.

The relative pronouns, according to *The Oxford English Grammar*, are *which*, *that*, and *who* or *whom*. Some people include certain uses of *where* and *when*, but most authorities don't. Relative pronouns introduce relative clauses:

> The computer, *which had stopped working*, was in the garbage.

> The machine *that he bought* was a piece of junk.

> The man, *whom she loved*, had betrayed her.

> Rudy, *who had always loved her*, committed suicide.

A relative clause postmodifies a noun. That's a fancy way of saying that it comes after a noun and describes it. So relative clauses are really modifiers that act like adjectives to describe, qualify, or limit some other word in the sentence.

In our first example, can you identify the noun that is being postmodified by the relative clause *which had stopped working*? It's *computer*. In the second sentence, the relative clause *that he bought* is modifying (qualifying) *the machine*. In the third sentence, the relative clause *whom she loved* modifies *the man*. And in the fourth sentence, the relative clause *who had always loved her* gives added description of *Rudy*.

Start seeing relative clauses as something akin to adjectives and start taking note of which word each relative clause points to, and you'll have a lot more power over how you use them. And remember, relative clauses are great tools for squeezing extra information into a sentence, but only if that information fits.

Compare these two sentences:

> The new schedule will help reduce crowds over the closing weekend, which is traditionally the busiest.

> The new schedule that will be implemented next year and that is the brainchild of Mr. Lawson, who founded the show in 1988, will help reduce the number of people who attend over the closing weekend, which is usually the biggest problem because it is traditionally the busiest weekend of the show that Lawson puts on.

That first example is fine. That second one needs to be broken up because our relative clauses are cramming in too much information:

> The new schedule is the brainchild of Mr. Lawson, who founded the show in 1988. The schedule will help reduce the number of people who attend over the closing weekend, which is traditionally the busiest.

This revision still has relative clauses. But with just one per sentence, it now reads well.

Now look at this sentence:

> He left early, which was fine by me.

Here, the relative clause that begins with *which* isn't pointing to a noun. It's pointing to a whole idea. These are sometimes called sentential relative clauses.

There are a few more things you should know about relative clauses, which I'll list here quickly before explaining each in full. First, relative clauses can be either restrictive or nonrestrictive. Second, this distinction is at the center of a controversy over how you can use the word *which*. Third, there exists something called the zero relative, which refers to the absence of a relative pronoun at the head of a relative clause. Fourth, sometimes it's easy to mistake a subordinating conjunction for a relative pronoun.

Restrictive and *nonrestrictive* refer to the job a clause performs in a sentence. A restrictive clause can't be removed from a sentence without harming the point of the main clause:

> Any house that I buy must be yellow.

The relative clause here is *that I buy*. To test whether it's restrictive or nonrestrictive, take it out. You end up with

> Any house must be yellow.

That just ain't so. And with the relative clause removed from our sentence, we can appreciate the big job it was doing. The relative clause told us which house must be yellow. Not just any house, but any house that I buy. Our clause takes the enormous group encompassed by *any house* and narrows it down—restricts it—to a smaller group: *houses I could buy*. Now compare that to

> The house, which has termites, is yellow.

You can lift the relative clause right out of this sentence without any loss of meaning to the main clause. The main clause says, *The house is yellow*. That's perfectly logical all by itself. The fact that it has termites is extra information. It doesn't further specify which house we're talking about. It's not essential to understanding our main clause. Therefore, *which has termites* is, in this sentence, a nonrestrictive relative clause.

And did you notice the commas? They're a big clue. The commas tell you that the information they set off is nonessential, often called parenthetical information. So restrictive relative clauses do not take commas but nonrestrictive relative clauses do.

Compare these two sentences:

> The ceremony will honor the athletes, who won.

> The ceremony will honor the athletes who won.

That little comma makes a world of difference. In the first sentence, *all* the athletes won. In the second sentence, we see that only some athletes won and they're the ones who will be honored. The difference hinges on just one comma because that comma signals whether the clause that follows is restrictive or nonrestrictive.

Most of us use relative clauses effectively every day without thinking about them. But full mastery of the art of sentence writing requires you to stop and take notice of the stunning power of restrictive and nonrestrictive clauses.

Restrictive relative clauses are sometimes called essential relative clauses because they're essential to understanding which thing is being talked about. They're also sometimes called defining clauses because they define which thing is being talked about. Those are all just different ways of saying the same thing.

And here comes our controversy: *The Associated Press Stylebook* and *The Chicago Manual of Style* tell their followers that *which* is only for nonrestrictive clauses. So according to them it would be wrong to say *Any house which I buy must be yellow*. Many disagree, arguing that this is a standard and perfectly fine use of *which*. For your purposes, just think of AP's and Chicago's "rule" as a style recommendation that you can choose to follow—or not. But don't be surprised if an editor changes your *which*es to *that*s.

Now, regarding the zero relative, compare these two sentences:

> George got the job that you wanted.

> George got the job you wanted.

This situation confounds a lot of writers. How do you know when to use *that*? If you're one of the writers who have puzzled over this, I have good news: it's up to you. Now that you know how to spot a relative clause, you can handle the news that relative pronouns are sometimes optional. When you leave them out, it's called the zero relative.

And remember, relative pronouns can do other jobs. *That* can, as we've seen, be a relative pronoun: *The apple that is best for pies is the Granny Smith.* But *that* can also be a pronoun: *I like that.* It can be an adjective: *That guy is cool.* It can be a subordinating conjunction: *That John ate was a fact that would torment him for thirty minutes as he watched the other kids frolicking in the pool.*

Especially important is the distinction between the relative pronoun *that* and the subordinating conjunction *that*. Remember: relative clauses are modifiers (just like adjectives) but subordinate clauses can be used as subjects and objects (just like nouns). To spot the difference, just determine whether the whole *that* clause is modifying a noun: *The family that stays together.* If so, it's a relative pronoun. If *that* is followed by a whole clause it's a subordinating conjunction: *That you love me is all I need to know. Harry learned that life is not fair.*

Like *that*, *who* can also do different jobs. In *the man, who was driving, is tall*, the *who* is a relative pronoun. But in *Who was driving?* it's not working to modify a noun. It's working as a personal pronoun.

You don't need to memorize every possible job these words can do. Just begin to notice their function in a sentence and how relative clauses function in well-written sentences.

If you're looking to distill all this stuff about relative clauses into a practical guideline to help your writing, consider this: Relative clauses seem to work best when they cast a little extra light on a thing or an idea. But they can quickly become a problem when they're used to insert history or backstory. They're at their worst when they contain an unstated "Oh, by the way" or "I never took the time to mention this before, so let me squeeze something in now."

Consider, too, that whenever you have more than one relative clause in a sentence, you might want to break the sentence up. Then again, like Gaiman, you might not. Just know that you have the choice.

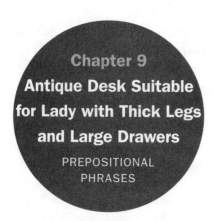

Chapter 9

Antique Desk Suitable for Lady with Thick Legs and Large Drawers

PREPOSITIONAL PHRASES

Grammar isn't all suffering. A simple Google search for the term *misplaced modifier* can prove that.

> Woman: They said it's going to rain on the radio.
> Man: Why would anyone leave a radio outside?

> A classified ad offered "Mixing bowl set designed to please cook with round bottom for efficient beating."

> I photographed an elephant in my pajamas.

> A superb and inexpensive restaurant; fine food expertly served by waitresses in appetizing forms.

> Have several very old dresses from grandmother in beautiful condition.

Prepositional phrases, like relative clauses, are modifiers. But they're more fun because they're so devious. It's easy to lose track of what you're saying with a prepositional phrase. But if you understand them for what they are—modifiers—your sentences will benefit tremendously. Let's start with the supposedly real classified ad mentioned in our chapter title:

> Antique desk suitable for lady with thick legs and large drawers.

The ad is funny because it sounds like *with thick legs and large drawers* is modifying *lady*. It's not. It's modifying *desk*. (At least, I hope it is.)

The ad is a noun phrase that contains numerous modifiers, one of which contains its own noun phrase. Let's look at all the pieces.

Antique is a straightforward adjective that comes before the noun. Easy. So let's set that aside.

Desk is a noun and the head of our noun phrase.

Suitable is an adjective. It comes after the noun, but that's okay. It's still an adjective and it's still modifying desk.

For lady is a prepositional phrase. The preposition is *for* and its object is the noun *lady*. Prepositional phrases can describe or define nouns—just as adjectives do. Or they can do the work of an adverbial, answering the questions *when, where, to what degree*, or *in what manner* or modifying verbs, adjectives, other adverbs, or whole thoughts. In our advertisement, *for lady* is modifying the adjective *suitable* just as a more straightforward adverb might: *extremely suitable, undeniably suitable*.

Suitable for lady modifies *desk*. There's nothing else it could be referring to. That's not true of our next prepositional phrase, *with thick legs and large drawers*.

See, here's the thing about modifiers: people usually expect them to modify the closest possible word, not one that's farther away in the sentence. When you write, *Derek had a pine armoire, a wooden bench, and a desk with thick legs and large drawers*, nobody is going to wonder whether the armoire or the bench had thick legs and large drawers. They're going to assume that this modifier is deliberately and correctly affixed to the noun closest to it. That's the Reader's expectation, and as writers we must be careful to accommodate it.

Our classified ad defies Reader expectation. It sets the modifier *with thick legs and large drawers* right next to *lady*, creating a very different image indeed.

Misplaced or poorly placed prepositional phrases can crop up in a lot of different sentence structures. But if you think of prepositional phrases as modifiers and keep your focus on the things they modify, you'll do fine.

Often, the fixes are very simple:

> Problem sentence: They said it's going to rain on the radio.
> Solution: Move the prepositional phrase *on the radio* closer
> to the verb it modifies: *said*.
> Improved sentence: They said on the radio that it's going
> to rain.

Problem sentence: I photographed an elephant in my pajamas.

Solution: Move the prepositional phrase *in my pajamas* closer to the pronoun it modifies: *I*.

Improved sentence: In my pajamas, I photographed an elephant.

Problem sentence: Fine food expertly served by waitresses in appetizing forms. (Note that this has two prepositional phrases, but the first one, *by waitresses*, clearly modifies *served*.)

Solution: Move the prepositional phrase *in appetizing forms* closer to the noun it modifies: *food*.

Improved sentence: Fine food in appetizing forms expertly served by waitresses.

Not all fixes are as easy.

In *mixing bowl set designed to please cook with round bottom for efficient beating*, we could just move our prepositional phrase to get *mixing bowl set with round bottom for efficient beating designed to please cook*. But now the modifier *designed to please cook* comes right after *beating*. Is that confusing? Perhaps not. But it's still a little weird. It's better to rewrite it. You could ditch the stuff about *designed to please cook*. That's already pretty clear. Or you could put it into another sentence: *Mixing bowl set with round bottom for efficient beating. Cooks love it.* Or perhaps *Designed to please cook: Mixing bowl set with round bottom for efficient beating.*

Prepositional phrases can also work mischief with lists. Readers know that sometimes one modifier can apply to everything in a list:

She sang "Fame," "The Promise," and "Lies" with great gusto.

Other times the modifier might refer to only the nearest noun:

Kirk ate ravioli, pizza, and strawberries with whipped cream.

We'll examine this dynamic more in chapter 15. Here, the important thing is to remember that prepositional phrases work a lot like adjectives and adverbs and your Reader has some pretty strong ideas about where they should go.

Chapter 10
Dangler Danger
PARTICIPLES
AND OTHER
DANGLERS

Running down the street in high heels, my dog was too fast for me to catch.

Really? Your dog wears high heels? That's hot.

Walking down the beach, my shoulders got sunburned.

How nice of your shoulders to give your feet a break from all that walking.

Stuffed with chestnuts, Peter served the turkey.

Why was Peter eating so many chestnuts right before dinner?

In the last chapter, we saw how prepositional phrases work as modifiers. In the chapter before that, we saw how relative clauses work as modifiers. In this chapter, we'll look at how participial units like *walking down the beach* and *stuffed with chestnuts* can also be modifiers. There's just one problem: no one knows whether we should call these units phrases or clauses.

And when I say no one, I mean no one.

Some expert sources, including *The Oxford English Grammar* and *The Cambridge Grammar of the English Language*, usually call these participial clauses. Other expert sources, including veteran grammar teacher and grammar-book author Laurie Rozakis, PhD, say they're phrases. Still other experts say the difference is just a matter of interpretation—theoretical stuff that doesn't affect how we handle them. One of these experts is *Cambridge Grammar of the English Language* coauthor Geoffrey Pullum. I e-mailed him myself to ask.

It's not about what you call them. It's about where you put them. Put one in the wrong place, and it qualifies as a misplaced modifier, just as prepositional phrases like *with round bottom for efficient beating* do.

A participle is a verb form that usually ends in *ing*, *ed*, or *en*. The *-ing* form is called the progressive participle. The *-ed* and *-en* forms are called past participles, though irregular verbs don't follow the pattern: *shown, brought, led, dealt, leapt, seen*, and so on, are all past participles. Past participles work with forms of *have* and progressive participles work with forms of *be* to form different verb conjugations: *We have walked, Joe is walking*, and so on.

But you can also use a participle to modify a noun—just like an adjective. Look at *painted* in *They have painted the wall* and *It's a painted wall*. In the first example, it's part of a verb. In the second, it is essentially an adjective. Another example: *Life has broken Henry* and *Henry is a broken man*.

A participial phrase or clause, then, is simply any participle that serves as a modifier. And it can do so with or without accessories:

Exhausted, Harry fell into bed.
Exhausted from the long hike, Harry fell into bed.

Speeding, Nanette hit a pole.
Speeding in her Ferrari, Nanette hit a pole.

Eating, Dave almost choked.
Eating pastrami, Dave almost choked.

Either way, a participial phrase or clause can be seen as a modifier. It modifies a noun or pronoun. So from our examples, who was exhausted? Harry. And who was speeding? Nanette. Harry and Nanette are the nouns being modified by those participial units.

Now identify what's wrong with this sentence:

Daydreaming about Nanette, Dan's foot went right into
a puddle.

Either Dan has one smart foot, or we have on our hands the legendary beast known as the dangling participle.

A dangling participle is simply a participle that seems to point to the wrong noun.

As we saw in our chapter on prepositional phrases, Readers usually expect a modifier to refer to the closest noun. That's why, in our last example, we're suggesting that Dan's foot was daydreaming and not Dan. To fix these, just make sure that you've chosen the right noun—for example, "Dan" instead of "foot"—and that the participial phrase or clause that's modifying it is as close as possible.

Daydreaming about Nanette, Dan stepped in a puddle.

You can also make your participial phrase or clause into a subordinate clause so it's no longer a modifier and therefore no longer has to be right next to whatever it's modifying:

> While Dan was daydreaming about Nanette, his foot went right into a puddle.

That's it. That's as hard it gets. Get past the fear of the grammar jargon and you see that dangling participles are very simple.

Participles aren't the only things that can dangle:

> A Kentucky Derby–winning colt, Thunderbolt's jockey was very proud.

Did you catch it? We just called the jockey a colt. This is a tricky one because it looks as though the colt, Thunderbolt, comes right after the modifier. But no. We didn't write *Thunderbolt*. We wrote *Thunderbolt's*, rendering it a modifier. In the noun phrase *Thunderbolt's jockey*, the headword is *jockey*, not *Thunderbolt's*.

There's one more danger with participles. Because some are identical to gerunds, they can get confusing:

> Visiting relatives can be fun.

Does this mean that the act of visiting (*visiting* as a gerund) can be fun, or that relatives who are visiting you (*visiting* as a modifier) can be fun? We don't know. Subtler examples crop up all the time in professional writing:

> Here are the trends leading interior designers and industry experts across the country have predicted will be hot this season.

After pausing, the Reader can see that *leading* is an adjective modifying *interior designers* and not an action being performed by *trends*. But it's usually best not to force the Reader to do a doubletake:

> Here are the trends *that* leading interior designers and industry experts across the country have predicted will be hot this season.

The best way to avoid danglers is to stay vigilant. After a while it becomes a working part of the brain. Considering how much this can help your sentences, it's worth the effort.

Chapter 11
The Writing Was Ignored by the Reader
PASSIVES

From time to time, a writer will post something like this on a writers' Internet message board:

> Help! I can't get this sentence out of the passive: "Emma was walking down the street."

The writer may add that she knows this sentence is passive because it has a form of *to be* (in this case *was*) coupled with a word that ends in *ing*: *walking.* There's just one problem. The sentence is not passive. Neither is this:

> Sue had been considering doing some thinking about being more accepting and becoming more loving.

Horrible, yes. Passive, no. At least, not in the sense we mean when we talk about the passive voice.

There are two myths about passives that we need to debunk right away:

1. Passive structure is bad.
2. Passive structure is any action-impaired sentence that uses an *-ing* or *-ed* verb with a form of *to be* (like *is* or *was*).

Caveats about passives have been overstated and distorted. Yes, passives can be awful. Yes, they're a serious problem for some novice writers. Yes, you need to be on the lookout for them. But this doesn't mean passives are always bad. They're quite useful when used wisely—indispensable, even. So here's how you should look at them. It will probably sound familiar: passive voice is a powerful tool in the hands of a skilled writer, but it's brain-numbing poison in the hands of an unskilled writer. So you should understand the concept and use the passive only by choice. Learn to recognize passive sentences so you can consider whether they would be better in the active voice.

Luckily, the concept is easy to master.

Here's the best way to understand passive voice: it occurs when the object of an action is made the grammatical subject of a sentence. (Technically, it's more precise to say that the passive occurs when the object of a transitive verb is made the subject of a sentence. But if that makes your eyes glaze over, stick with the first definition.) Compare these two sentences:

Ned made the coffee.

The coffee was made by Ned.

In the first example, we have someone performing an action, followed by the action itself, followed by the thing being acted upon: *subject* + *verb* + *object*. In the second example, the thing being acted upon, the object, is made the subject of our sentence. That's passive structure. Let's look at some more examples:

> Active: Becky threw the ball.
> Passive: The ball was thrown by Becky.
>
> Active: Manny gave Ralph the gun.
> Passive: The gun was given to Ralph by Manny.
>
> Active: Everybody loves pasta.
> Passive: Pasta is loved by everybody.
>
> Active: The monster ate Victoria.
> Passive: Victoria was eaten by the monster.

Any of the passives in these examples might be the best choice under certain circumstances. That last one in particular seems to work well in its passive form.

Now that we understand passives, we know that our first example, *Emma was walking*, isn't passive, because Emma is both the doer of the action and the grammatical subject of the sentence.

Let's practice. Convert the following passive sentences into active form:

> The cake was baked by Rodney.
>
> The compliments were appreciated by the hostess.
>
> The money was stolen.

Okay, that was sneaky of me. I threw in that last one to illustrate an important point: Often, a passive construction will contain a nice little *by* phrase that tells you who or what is performing the action.

But that *by* phrase is optional. Writers often drop it. And you can't convert the sentence into active form unless you know who or what should be your new sentence's subject. You can change the first two into active voice because we know that Rodney baked the cake and the hostess appreciated the compliments. But we don't know who stole the money.

If we really want to make this sentence active, we can come up with a subject. We can say J*udy stole the money* if we know for a fact that Judy did it. If we don't know, we can say *someone stole the money* or *a thief stole the money.* But in a situation like this, the best option is often to leave the sentence in the passive. In fact, that's when passives are best: anytime you want to downplay the doer of an action.

The president was re-elected emphasizes the president in a way that an active form such as *The voters re-elected the president* does not. In the first sentence, you're talking about the president. In the second, you're talking about voters, which may not be what you want.

Sometimes, passives are the greatest thing in the world:

> Professor Persimmon is considered a leading economic expert.

> Meryl Streep is widely regarded as one of the greatest actors of her generation.

Taking those out of the passive would change the character of the sentences considerably:

> People consider Professor Persimmon an expert.

> American moviegoers regard Meryl Streep as one of the greatest actors of her generation.

These flip-flops put the focus in a different place entirely. They call attention to the missing information, leading to questions like What people? Which moviegoers? Who are these folks who get to decide such things, and why didn't anybody ask my opinion?

By de-emphasizing these issues, passives let a writer be sneaky. For example, if a writer is too lazy to actually find out Professor Persimmon's credentials, a passive *is considered* can be a convenient weasel-like way to make unsubstantiated assertions.

But, once again, we come right back to our guiding light of Reader-serving writing. Sidestepping certain questions—like Who anointed Professor Persimmon a leading expert?—can be a fine way to keep the focus where it needs to be in order to best serve the Reader. If your article is about the economy, there's probably no reason you must spend time discussing your economist's credentials or who bestowed them on him. If you're working in the Reader's best interest and have thus earned his trust, you don't have to verify every value judgment your story might make. You can get on to more relevant information instead. In that case, a passive sentence about Persimmon's credentials is just fine.

Let's do two more quick practice sentences. Convert these into active form:

> Kevin was being watched.

> Kevin was being coy.

How'd you do? Your answer for the first one should look something like *Someone was watching Kevin* or *Nelson was watching Kevin* or *The voyeur was watching Kevin*. Your answer for the second one—well, as you may have guessed, it was a trick question.

The first sentence is passive. The second one is not. Remember our simple definition of passive voice: when the object of an action is made the grammatical subject of the sentence. We can easily see that an action is taking place in our first sentence and Kevin is on the receiving end of it. He's the doee, not the doer.

But the second sentence, though structured almost identically, does not make Kevin the object of an action. Someone is watching him, but no one is coying him. *Coy* is an adjective, not an action. That is, though *watch* is a transitive verb, *coy* isn't a verb at all. Therefore the second sentence is not passive. It's active.

All this leads to the question of how, exactly, you form passives.

You just use a form of *to be* as something called an auxiliary combined with something *The Oxford English Grammar* calls the *passive participle*, which is identical to the past participle. As we saw in the last chapter, participles are pieces of conjugated verbs. Past participles are the pieces that usually end in *ed* or *en*:

> In the past you have walked.

> On that morning, you had woken.

Irregular verb participles often don't end in *ed* or *en*:

> woken (past participle of wake)
> driven (past participle of drive)
> drunk (past participle of drink)
> spoken (past participle of speak)
> risen (past participle of rise)
> thought (past participle of think)
> lain (past participle of lie)

But whether your verb is regular or irregular, forming a passive is simple. Just flip-flop the doer and the doee in your sentence and insert an auxiliary *to be* before a passive participle:

> Larry watched Kevin.
>
> Kevin was [auxiliary] watched [passive participle] by Larry.

Even if your active sentence already contains a form of *to be* as an auxiliary, it's the same idea. Just flip-flop the doer and the doee and insert another auxiliary *to be* before a passive participle:

> Larry *was* watching Kevin [active sentence with form of *to be* as auxiliary]
>
> Kevin *was being* watched by Larry [passive sentence with inserted auxiliary, *being*, working with original auxiliary, *was*]

That's more analysis than instruction, by the way. No one ever stops and says, "Now what's that dang formula for making passives again?" Passives come pretty naturally, even to people who have no idea what a participle is. So don't worry about the mechanics. Just start recognizing passive sentences and considering whether they would be better in active form. The answer can be subjective. But the passives that writing pros consider bad are the ones that squelch interesting action.

Tim was shot by Barbara is anemic compared to *Barbara shot Tim*. The latter has a sense of immediacy and power. Passive forms dilute that power. In our active form, the action is the verb. In passive form, the verb emphasizes being more than doing. That's what people mean when they say that passives are bad. Yes, their point is overstated, but there's a big lump of truth at its center. Passives often stink:

> After he had been flown to Chicago and had been checked into his hotel room, he was called on the phone by his boss.

Sometimes, the best way to fix bad passives is to restructure the passage:

> His company flew him to Chicago. After he arrived and checked into his hotel room, his boss called.

Bringing a passive sentence to life is that easy.

Chapter 12

You Will Have Been Conjugating

OTHER MATTERS OF TENSE

As we saw in the last chapter, a lot of the sentences people think are passive really aren't. But, with surprising frequency, these deceptively active sentences are nonetheless very bad:

> Albert had been wanting to start saving and investing but, being caring, he was considering giving his savings to the woman he was seeing.

To avoid horrible sentences like this, we need to go beyond the simple concept of passive voice. We must get a better understanding of verbs and verb tenses. The following chart contains the basic tenses. You don't need to memorize their names. But you should read them at least once and note how they show when something happened and whether the action has been completed.

The progressive, which some call continuous, shows ongoing action. The progressive uses a form of *to be*, such as *is*, *was*, or *are* as an auxiliary—a helper.

The perfect shows that something is fully completed either by the time you're talking about it or by the time indicated. The perfect uses a form of *have* as an auxiliary.

TENSE	EXAMPLE
Simple present	*I walk*
Simple past	*I walked*
Future	*I will walk (or I am going to walk)*
Present progressive	*I am walking*
Past progressive	*I was walking*
Future progressive	*I will be walking*
Present perfect	*I have walked*
Past perfect	*I had walked*
Future perfect	*I will have walked*
Present perfect progressive	*I have been walking*
Past perfect progressive	*I had been walking*
Future perfect progressive	*I will have been walking*

A lot of writers get confused about which verb tense to use. Remember, all this jargon and analysis is rooted in simple common sense. For example, which do you think makes the best first sentence for a story?

The grandmother didn't want to go to Florida.

The grandmother hadn't been wanting to go to Florida.

The grandmother hasn't been wanting to go to Florida.

The grandmother isn't wanting to go to Florida.

The grandmother will not have been wanting to go to Florida.

The first example is the opening sentence of Flannery O'Connor's "A Good Man is Hard to Find." The others are examples of how bad verb tenses might have destroyed O'Connor's career. These sentences are busy, they're abstract, they're a little confusing, and they take longer to get to the point. Of course, there are times when these convoluted tenses capture your meaning and mood exactly. But it's obvious that often the simplest verb tense is the best verb tense.

Most straight news stories are written in the simple past tense. The reason: They tell of things that happened. For example, looking at the front page of the April 24, 2009, *Los Angeles Times*, I see stories that begin with

> The Obama administration agreed . . .
> [*agreed* = simple past tense]
>
> Emboldened Taliban fighters imposed control . . .
> [*imposed* = simple past tense]
>
> The nation's consumer-in-chief made himself pointedly clear . . .
> [*made* = simple past tense]

All these sentences tell of things that happened. Simple past. But, looking at the same *Los Angeles Times* page, I also see these openers:

> The Obama administration is preparing to admit into the United States . . . [*is preparing* = present progressive]
>
> Sets Tomita pauses at Manzanar's southwest boundary and scans the high desert . . . [*pauses* = simple present; *scans* = simple present]

The reason behind the first example is simple: The news article wasn't reporting something that had happened. It was reporting something that was happening—the preparations were continuing—even as the reader was learning about them.

The second example is not as simple. For this long feature article, the writer chose to start off in the present tense, even though Sets Tomita had already finished his pausing and scanning long before reporter Pete Thomas sat at his keyboard to write about it. Why, then, is this past event written about in the present tense? Because the writer chose it as a creative device. No doubt, he felt that bringing the Reader into the moment would enrich the Reader's experience. There was no need to tell the Reader, "Even though it sounds like this is going on right now, it actually happened days ago." The Reader knows that. He knows he's been invited along on a journey. Would he enjoy it more if it were written in the past tense? Who's to say? Thomas gambled that the present tense would work best, and if his editors and copy editors disagreed, it never would have made it into the newspaper that way.

Fiction, too, is often written in the past tense. Novelists and short story writers sometimes choose the present tense, usually for the same reason we saw in the last example: the present tense carries an in-the-moment urgency not found in past tenses, so it's a valid creative device.

Yet, despite this obvious benefit, the present tense is surprisingly unpopular in professional writing. In *You've Got to Read This*, an anthology of thirty-five short stories by some of fiction's most acclaimed writers, only five of the stories are in the present tense. Of the remaining thirty, a few start out with some overview information in the present tense, like John Updike's "Packed Dirt, Churchgoing, a Dying Cat, a Traded Car," which begins, "Different things move us." But after two paragraphs Updike shifts to the past tense with a simple adverbial device: "Last night." That's where the real story begins.

The five stories not in the past tense tend to be short and some have an experimental feel, like Jamaica Kincaid's "Girl," which is just one and a half pages long, comprises just a single sentence, and is written primarily in the imperative—that is, in commands: "Wash the white clothes on Monday and put them on the stone heap; wash the color clothes on Tuesday and put them on the clothesline to dry . . ."

We can only guess why thirty of the writers told their stories in the past tense. Maybe it's just too hard to keep up the level of intensity created by the present tense. Maybe they felt that present tense is too demanding on the Reader, perhaps even tiring. Maybe they felt it would have distracted from their stories. Maybe they wanted a plain-vanilla traditional vehicle for telling their stories because they were more interested in the story itself than in playing with conventions of form.

Present-tense storytelling is even rarer in longer forms—for example, in the novel. If present-tense intensity is hard to maintain for ten pages, it's probably about thirty times harder to maintain for three hundred pages.

I can't tell you which tense to choose for your writing. No one can. But there's much to be learned by professional writers' choices. Simple past tense is the standard form. It's a safe choice. You can deviate from it, but unless you have a good reason to, maybe you shouldn't.

So far, we've been looking at straightforward tenses: simple past, present progressive, and simple present. But what about more complex tenses?

> Tommy Q. Public *was applying* to law school. [past progressive]

> Jane Doe *had been making* breakfast when she heard the crash. [past perfect progressive]

Obviously, these tenses can be indispensable and have a place in both fiction and nonfiction. In fiction, especially, if a writer can pull it off, she's free to load up her stories with stuff like

> Pilly Bilgrim *will have been becoming* unstuck in time.
> [future perfect progressive]

But even writers who want to avoid these tenses should understand how they function.

As explained in *The Complete Idiot's Guide to Grammar and Style*, the past perfect is used for an "action completed before another." The past perfect progressive is used for a "continuing action interrupted by another." The future perfect progressive is for a "continuing future action done before another."

Notice how these all mention "another"? These complex verb tenses tell when one action took place relative to when another took place:

> After having been rejected by NASA and Caltech, Lucky got a job at McDonald's.

The verb tenses tell us that Lucky got the McDonald's job after the other two places shot him down. But they tell us something more. We know that *Lucky got a job* is the big event in this sentence.

After having been rejected is something that happened relative to that big moment. So verb tenses, like subordination, tell the Reader what information is most important. *Amy had been going to the same beauty parlor for twenty years* begs to be followed by *when*, as in *when her hair fell out.*

This is why past-tense stories are told primarily in the simple past tense and why present-tense stories stick mainly to the simple present tense: because every alternative flies in the face of the Reader's expectations. Readers expect the simple-tense stuff to be the main story. The stuff in more complicated tenses is presumed to relate other events to that main story's timeline.

Can you defy these expectations, play with verb tenses, look for other approaches, and use experimental methods in your writing? Sure. If you can pull it off. Just remember that in those thirty-five short stories, none of the writers from Welty to Kafka even bothered to try. And there's a good reason why no Dickens novel begins, "It had been being the best of times, it had been being the worst of times."

Usually, you can shift from a more complex tense to a simple one after just one sentence:

> Valerie had slept for hours. She dreamed about wild horses and smoke signals.

The first sentence is past perfect. But for the second sentence the writer shifted to simple past tense. That's okay because the Reader gets it. The first sentence is all you need to anchor this story at a point in time. Sure, the writer could have continued with the past perfect tense:

> Valerie had slept for hours. She had dreamed about wild horses and smoke signals. She had woken several times when she had heard noises. But the noises had been nothing more than the wind. She had realized this quickly and had fallen back asleep right away. Only after she had had a full night's sleep had she finally gotten out of bed.

That's grammatically fine yet borderline unreadable. You can tell that a shift to the past is coming. It has to. No story can go on like this. So there's no reason to delay the switch from past perfect to simple past. Might as well get it out of the way sooner rather than later:

> Valerie had slept for hours. She dreamed about wild horses and smoke signals. She woke up several times when she heard noises. But the noises were nothing more than the wind. She realized this quickly and fell back asleep right away. Only after she had a full night's sleep did she finally get out of bed.

Let's look at another passage that shifts to a simple tense:

> The rain had been falling for days. It pummeled Chuck's bedroom window.

We could have stuck with the past perfect for our second sentence. But there was no reason to. The Reader had received his time cue. So it was okay to shift into "and from there our story gets under way" mode.

Not all tense shifts are as smooth:

> Umberto was an excellent wrestler who is kind and always eager to be helpful.

This is what people mean by a bad tense shift. It's clearly a mistake. The writer lost track of the time period she was writing about. It's a common problem, but it's pretty easy to avoid. Just remember the *when* of your story and remember to be consistent and logical.

Sometimes tense combinations can be tricky. For example, compare

> Copernicus was thrilled when he discovered that the earth revolves around the sun.

to

> Copernicus was thrilled when he discovered that the earth revolved around the sun.

Which is right? They both are. But the first one is better.

It is true that the earth *revolved* around the sun. It is also true that the earth *revolves* around the sun. But which is more notable to the Reader? Well, Copernicus's discovery wasn't true only back then, nor has it lost its significance. It informs our science to this day. That's why most would agree that the continuing revolving is even more notable than the revolving that was going on in Copernicus's day.

All the verb tenses and even the passive voice are tools you can use anytime that they work. But simple past tense and active voice are safe choices that can save you anytime you get into trouble.

Nominalization is a simple concept, and taking a few moments to master it could help your writing tremendously. Consider this sentence:

> The walking of the dog was the difficulty from which Sherry's laziness had its emergence.

In this sentence, *walking, difficulty, laziness,* and *emergence* all work as nouns. But *walking* and *emergence* are rooted in verbs: *to walk* and *to emerge. Laziness* and *difficulty* are rooted in adjectives: *lazy* and *difficult.*

These are often called nominalizations. A nominalization is a form of a verb or an adjective that functions as a noun. Some call them buried verbs. Still others say that the ones that end in *ing*—called gerunds—don't qualify as nominalizations. But they can all hurt your writing in the same way, so we'll look at them all together. Here are some examples of the dreaded beasts called nominalizations:

> utilization (from the verb *utilize*)
> happiness (from the adjective *happy*)
> movement (from the verb *move*)
> lying (from the verb *lie*)
> persecution (from the verb *persecute*)
> dismissal (from the verb *dismiss*)
> fabrication (from the verb *fabricate*)
> atonement (from the verb *atone*)
> creation (from the verb *create*)
> intensity (from the adjective *intense*)
> cultivation (from the verb *cultivate*)
> refusal (from the verb *refuse*)
> incarceration (from the verb *incarcerate*)

Obviously, these are all legitimate words. They become a problem only when a writer uses them in place of more interesting actions or descriptions. Nine times out of ten, *Barb was happy* is better than *Barb had happiness* or *Barb exhibited happiness*.

Nominalizations are worst when an unskilled writer puts them into the form *the + gerund + of.* As we just saw, a gerund is the form of a verb that ends in *ing* and is used as a noun. Outside of a sentence, gerunds are indistinguishable from participles.

> Singing is hard [*singing* as a subject = gerund]

> She was singing [*singing* as part of verb phrase = participle]

Combined with a *the* and *of,* gerunds can be really bad news:

The singing of the song

The considering of the job offer

The walking of the dog

The knowing of the facts

The remembering of the appointment

You can see why structures like these don't show up much in Pulitzer-winning novels. They're wordy, they turn an action into an inanimate object, and they downplay the doer of the action. On rare occasions, this is exactly what you want. More often it's just terrible writing. You see a big improvement if you just pare these structures down to their base gerund form.

The singing of "Funky Town" is part of the ceremony.
= Singing "Funky Town" is part of the ceremony.

The walking of the dog is good exercise.
= Walking the dog is good exercise.

The knowing of the facts will help your test score.
= Knowing the facts will help your test score.

The remembering of the appointment is crucial.
= Remembering the appointment is crucial.

Usually, you're better off recasting the sentence to make the gerunds into real actions with real actors:

> The bride and groom sing "Funky Town" as part of the ceremony.
>
> Phil walks his dog and it's good exercise.
>
> You should know the facts. It will help your test score.
>
> It's crucial that you remember the appointment.

Gerunds aren't the only nominalized forms that work with *the* and *of* this way. Nominalizations rooted in adjectives can, too.

> The happiness of the bride
>
> The intensity of the staring
>
> The blatantness of the flirting

While these are better than the gerund examples earlier, they're still pretty bad.

When you fix a nominalization, you turn the real action into the main verb and you get to bring in the person or thing doing the action.

> The happiness of the bride was evident.
> = The bride was happy. That was evident.
>
> The refusal of the gift was shocking.
> = Vanessa refused the gift. I was shocked.

Bob's acquittal by the jury took place Monday.

= On Monday the jury acquitted Bob.

I appreciate Trevor's support.

= Trevor supports me and I appreciate it.

Notice how, in that last example, the nominalized form might be preferable. That goes to show you that a nominalization can be an excellent choice. But it can also be a terrible choice. So keep an eye out for nominalizations. Think of each as an opportunity— a chance to consider alternative, possibly better ways to structure your sentence. Sometimes you'll find that recasting them in simple subject-plus-verb form can make a better experience for the Reader. Sometimes you'll want to leave them as they are.

But don't write off all nominalizations as bad. Without them, this whole chapter couldn't have existed, because *nominalization* is itself a nominalization.

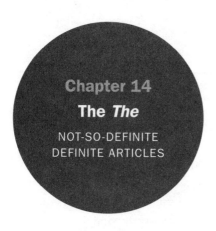

Look, there's a cat.

Look, there's the cat.

Ever stop to think about the word *the*? It's a tiny word, yet it's huge. It carries so much responsibility. It leans so heavily on your Reader. It says, "You're expected to know what I'm talking about." I guess that's why it's so annoying when a writer hasn't done her due diligence before dumping this expectation on you.

Katie screamed and grabbed the diary.

This is rock-solid writing if and only if you've addressed the question *what* diary? If you've mentioned somewhere earlier in the story that there exists a diary—if you've introduced it—*the diary* is fine. But if this is the first mention of the diary, that little *the* sends a bad message to the Reader. It says, "You know. The diary. The one I told you about." Even though you've done no such thing.

It's rude.

We all understand the basic idea of *the* without having to think about it. We get it intuitively. Unfortunately, all too often novice writers become lost in the information they're trying to convey and forget themselves. This is understandable. If you've been concocting a story involving a diary, that diary is very familiar to you. You know it intimately in a way that only a creator can. You know what condition the cover is in. You know whether it has a lock. You know what words are written inside and whether those words have the power to hurt or even to kill. To you, it's no longer just *a* diary. It's *the* diary—the one you've pictured and pondered and imbued with life-changing importance. When you finally start to put this thing you created into words, you have to step outside your head far enough to remember that the Reader hasn't spent the last year or two getting cozy with *the* diary. It's the writer's job to put it in the Reader's hands—to bridge the gap between a state of unknowing and a state of knowing. That's what writing *is*.

The same applies to nonfiction writers. But unlike the novelist or short story writer who imagined the diary, the nonfiction writer may have actually *seen* the diary. The writer has a huge amount of information that the Reader does not—everything from the color to the size to the coffee cup rings on the diary cover to the crisp neatness of the handwriting within. To the nonfiction writer, it is unmistakably *the* diary. But she has some work to do before she can make the Reader feel some of the intimacy that makes it more than just *a* diary.

Of course, there are ways to reconcile a *the* before an unfamiliar item. The best way is to explain immediately after the item. One of the best devices for doing this is a relative clause. Relative clauses, which we know postmodify nouns, can come soon after a word to add description or clarity to it:

> Katie screamed and grabbed the diary that her mother had
> given her.

Ta-da! The little relative clause *that her mother had given her* tells the reader more than just who gave Katie the diary. It tells the Reader, "Here's your explanation. Here's what you need to know to be up to speed on this diary. Here's why you can now feel some ownership of it, why you can now think of it not as *a* diary but as *the* diary."

I realize this is a lot of rumination about one little word, but this stuff is worth thinking about. For one thing, *the* cuts straight to the heart of Reader-serving writing. A badly used *the* happens because the writer got too wrapped up in what she was trying to say and forgot to be sensitive to the person she was saying it to.

And if you doubt that *the* has unique importance, consider this: It's the only word in the English language that is its own part of speech. It's in a category all its own.

The is called the definite article. It's distinct from *a* and *an*, which are called indefinite articles, and it's distinct from *this* and *these*, which are called demonstratives.

The stands alone.

So, now that I've thoroughly slammed using *the* to refer to stuff heretofore unknown to the Reader, how can we explain an all-too-common use of *the* like the one found in the very first sentence of the novel *Travels in the Scriptorium*, by Paul Auster?

> The old man sits on the edge of the narrow bed, palms spread out on his knees, head down, staring at the floor.

Auster has not yet introduced the old man. He didn't say *an old man*. He didn't say *there is an old man*. He hasn't told us there exists an old man, or a bed or a floor either, for that matter. This is the first sentence of the whole novel. The *the* suggests that we've already been introduced to the character and his surroundings, even though we have not. Yet it simply does not have the power to irk the Reader the way our diary did. What's up with that?

Simple. It's the flip side of the same coin. If *the* suggests familiarity, then putting *the* in front of something so surely unfamiliar suggests that familiarity will come. It foreshadows. It teases. The Reader knows that the writer is going to explain who *the old man* is. The writer is asking for the Reader's trust and promising something in return. It's a great device that skillful writers use all the time. It demonstrates the power of *the*. And it illustrates the importance of staying attuned to your Reader.

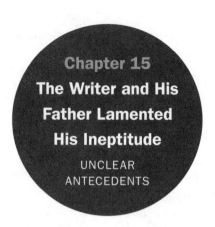

Chapter 15

The Writer and His Father Lamented His Ineptitude

UNCLEAR ANTECEDENTS

In the title of this chapter, "The Writer and His Father Lamented His Ineptitude," it's clear that someone is inept. The problem is we don't know who. *His* could refer to the writer or to his father. In the context of this book, it's a safe bet that we would be more focused on the writer. So we can guess that Sonny Boy is the one being slammed in this sentence. But the grammar doesn't confirm this. So we can't be sure. The possibility remains it could be Dad whose shortcomings are being lamented.

This problem is called an unclear antecedent. At its worst, this problem can completely ruin a written work:

> As the sheriff and the bandit fired their guns, a bullet pierced his heart. He fell to the ground. He was dead.

From the first sentence, we can't know whether it was the good guy or the bad guy who died. From the sentences that follow, it's clear that it will take a while for us to find out. Maybe we never will.

The passage is confusing and annoying and can be enough to make a Reader close a book or put down a manuscript forever.

Happily, these problems are easy to avoid. First, remember the lessons of our chapter on *the*. The Reader isn't in your head. Second, remember to pay careful attention to your pronouns—especially on the reread. This includes

- subject pronouns: *I, you, he, she, it, we, they*
- object pronouns: *me, you, him, her, it, us, them*
- possessive pronouns: *mine, yours, his, hers, its, ours, theirs*
- possessive determiners (think of these as adjective forms of possessive pronouns): *my, your, his, her, its, our, their*
- relative pronouns: *that, which, who, whom*

Of course, the first-person forms like *I* and *me* don't pack as much danger as third-person forms like *his, her, hers, their, theirs,* and so on. That's because usually fewer people could be *I* than could be *he*. So there's less chance of confusion.

Don't let the term *unclear antecedent* intimidate you. It means exactly what it sounds like: that it's unclear which prior thing is being referred to. In *Bubba lost his car keys*, the word *his* is a possessive determiner. Its antecedent—the thing to which it refers—is Bubba. So the Reader can see that you're talking about Bubba's keys.

For pronouns like *he* and *his*, unclear antecedents are very easy to create. You know whether it was the sheriff or the bandit who got shot, you just forgot that the Reader does not. It can happen to anyone. Just be sure to catch them when you reread your work. Make it a habit to scrutinize every *him, her,* and so on, to be sure they're clear.

When they're not, they're easy to fix:

> As the sheriff and the bandit fired their guns, a bullet pierced ~~his~~ the bandit's heart. He fell to the ground. He was dead.

Notice that we left *he* in the last two sentences. It's clear that *he* is the bandit. The Reader gets that.

Of course, we can imagine scenarios in which that *he* might not be so clear. If the bandit got shot just two sentences after the sheriff got shot, then it may not be clear at all to your Reader which one fell to the ground. But again, see how the Reader is your guiding light? It's almost as though he is helping *you.* Call it paradox, call it karma, call it a variation on AA members' belief that helping others helps them stay sober. Whatever. Just remember its power.

Not all pronouns are as easy to work with as personal pronouns like *he* and *him.* Take *it.* Unlike pronouns that refer to specific people, the pronoun *it* can refer to vague things like ideas. Compare these two uses of *it*:

> The car is parked. It is in a handicapped space.

> Jenna knows math. It is why she landed this job.

It is a pronoun like any other. It stands in for a noun. In the first example, the antecedent of *it* is clearly *the car.* But in our second example, what noun, exactly, does *it* represent? Jenna? Nope. Math? Nope. That leaves just *knows,* but that's a conjugated verb—an action under way. How can a pronoun refer to a verb? Easy: if, in the writer's head, *it* stands in for *knowing,* then that's what *it* means. The antecedent is implied. It could be the gerund *knowing,* as in, *Knowing math is why Jenna landed this job.* It could be an implied noun like

The fact that Jenna knows math is why she landed the job or *Jenna's knowledge of math is why she landed the job.*

That and *which* are two other pronouns that create problems:

> I went to the movies with my daughter, and though we were late, we caught most of the new Woody Allen movie. That's what life is all about.

What is what life is all about? Spending time with your daughter? Being late? Grabbing what you can out of a bad situation? Woody Allen? The slice of life created by combining all these elements? The writer should be clearer:

> I went to the movies with my daughter, and though we were late, we caught most of the new Woody Allen movie. ~~That's~~ <u>Afternoons like that are</u> what life is all about.

> I went to the movies with my daughter, and though we were late, we caught most of the new Woody Allen movie. ~~That's~~ <u>Grabbing what you can is</u> what life is all about.

This lesson extends beyond pronouns:

> Health care and education are among the fields that have added jobs. The audiovisual industry is, too.

This isn't wrong per se, but it causes me to do a double take. The audiovisual industry is *what*? It takes a moment to realize that the writer omitted part of the second sentence. The industry is *among the fields*. There's nothing wrong with leaving things implied as long as the implication is clear and doesn't make your Reader stumble:

> Kelly is crazy. Ryan is, too.

Implications only work if the Reader gets them. We don't say what Ryan *is*. We leave it implied. Yet it's perfectly clear. He's crazy.

When I look at the prior example about health care and education, what's most interesting to me is how the writer set herself up for trouble. Had she aimed for something less wordy than that whole *are among the* structure, the sentence would have been clear.

> The ~~H~~health care and education ~~are among the~~ fields ~~that~~ have added jobs. The audiovisual industry ~~is~~ has, too.

Whenever you use a pronoun or leave a noun merely implied, just be sure it's clear what you're talking about. If there's any doubt, say outright whatever you had wanted to imply. Returning to an earlier example:

> As the sheriff and the bandit fired their guns, a bullet pierced ~~his~~ the bandit's heart. He fell to the ground. He was dead.

A lot of writers avoid stuff like this because they worry it sounds redundant. By all means, if you can find alternative wording you like, use it:

> As the sheriff and the bandit fired their guns, a bullet pierced ~~his~~ the criminal's heart. He fell to the ground. He was dead.

> As Sheriff B. A. Ramirez and the bandit Stealy O'Reilly fired their guns, a bullet pierced the Irishman's shamrock-shaped

heart. He fell to the ground, spilling his bottle of Guinness. He was dead as the corpse in *Finnegans Wake*. There'd be no pot of gold at the end of his rainbow—no sweet bowl of Lucky Charms with its yellow moons, orange stars, and green clovers.

You get the idea.

Pick any wording you choose. But when you can find no synonyms or other embellishments to point squarely at your antecedent, repetitiveness is better than chaos. It's better to repeat the word *bandit* than to refuse to tell your Reader which one of your pivotal characters met his demise.

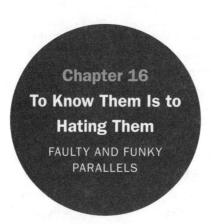

Sammy's Grill is open daily for lunch and dinner and Sunday brunch.

Sunday brunch daily? Awesome.

Roger praised the band's vocalist, bassist, drummer, keyboard, and guitar players.

That was sweet of Roger to praise the keyboard.

Relax in the lounge, the sauna, or by the pool.

Why just relax in the pool or by the pool when you can relax in by the pool?

She was awarded a national book award in fiction as well as a finalist for the Pulitzer Prize.

I wonder which prize finalist they gave her and what she did with him.

These are all real faulty parallels by real writers who were getting paid real money. They prove that parallels can be tricky. So it's worth taking a minute to master them.

Parallel form relies on Reader expectations. When Readers see something in list form, they expect it to be a list:

> Pablo has visited Maine, Idaho, Pennsylvania, Georgia, and New Jersey.

When you include an element that doesn't work like the others, you betray those expectations:

> Pablo has visited Maine, Idaho, Pennsylvania, loves Georgia, and New Jersey.

Parallels can be lists of words, phrases, or whole clauses. Each element should be in the same form and should attach in the same way to any shared phrase or clause. Look at this example:

> This car runs fast, lasts long, requires little maintenance, and holds its value.

The shared element is *this car*. Each of the listed items is a verb phrase that, on its own, can make *this car* a complete sentence. They all attach to *this car* in the same way. That would not work if one of the items was not a verb phrase, like *well* in this example:

> This car runs fast, well, lasts long, requires little maintenance, and holds its value.

Our structure suggests we meant, *This car runs fast, runs well, runs lasts long, runs requires little maintenance, and runs holds its value.* But that's not what we meant at all.

There are several ways to fix faulty parallels. You can add bits to the parallel items until they're equals:

> This car runs fast, *runs* well, lasts long, requires little mainte-
> nance, and holds its value.

Or you can break up the sentence in a way that signals that the list has ended:

> This car runs fast, well, and long, *and it* requires little mainte-
> nance and holds its value.

Parallels don't have to be faulty to be jarring:

> I was entertained by the decor, as well as the live piano
> music.

You could argue that *entertained by* applies to both the listed items. But it would be clearer if you repeated the *by*.

> I was entertained by the decor, as well as *by* the live piano
> music.

Every parallel poses its own unique dangers. There's no simple formula for getting it right every time. All you can do is proceed with caution and remember the Reader.

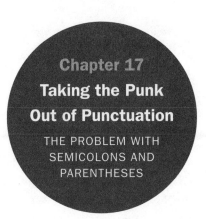

Chapter 17

Taking the Punk Out of Punctuation

THE PROBLEM WITH SEMICOLONS AND PARENTHESES

If you've come to this chapter looking for a balanced and reasonable discussion of semicolons and parentheses, keep looking. You'll find no balance here. I hate semicolons. I hate them so much that, even though I admit that they can be useful—lifesavers even—I'm comfortable saying that I hate them. I hate parentheses almost as much. They, too, have their place. In fact, I use them. As a Reader, I sometimes enjoy the effect they can create. Yet these reasonable observations don't mean I'm reasonable on the subject. I've seen too many writers abuse these punctuation marks too many times. I can't let go. I won't.

I suppose this is the very nature of prejudice—isolated bad experiences leading to broad and unfair overgeneralizations. But here we are, with me outright hating semicolons and parentheses even as I prepare to discuss them in terms that I hope will let you draw your own conclusions.

We'll start with an open airing of my biases:

1. Semicolons often serve no purpose other than to show off that the writer knows how to use semicolons.
2. Parentheses often let a writer cram in information she was too lazy to explain in a more Reader-friendly manner.

Aah. Feels good to get that off my chest. Now we can take a more academic approach.

Semicolons have two main jobs. First, they help manage unwieldy lists. Second, they separate two closely related clauses that could stand on their own as sentences. This first job doesn't bother me so much. That's because, sometimes, this semicolon really is a Reader-serving punctuation mark:

> Brad visited Pasadena, California; Cheyenne, Wyoming; Sarasota, Florida; and Boulder, Colorado.

These semicolons separate items that contain commas within them. The semicolons work like übercommas. Try replacing them with plain-old commas and you can see that they're crucial for making sense of this sentence. Without the semicolons, *Pasadena*, *California*, *Cheyenne*, and *Wyoming* would be equally weighted. If this sentence were read aloud, these words would be read in the same tone and with identical emphasis. The semicolons allow us to clearly see the groupings within our list—that is, that *Pasadena* and *California* make up one thing and are not two things.

And that's the last nice thing you'll hear me say about semicolons.

This function of the semicolon, while crucial in some situations, gets abused. That is, it gives writers an excuse—nay, an incentive—to write obnoxious sentences:

> He wanted to visit Brooklyn, New York; Queens, New York; and Schenectady, New York, and he had already invited his cousin, Pete; his mother's next-door neighbor, Rob; and the neighborhood dog, a terrier, to join him.

This writer is too enamored of her semicolons. She uses them at the expense of her sentence. She would be better off using none.

> He wanted to visit Brooklyn, Queens, and Schenectady. He had already invited his cousin, Pete, his next-door neighbor, Rob, and a local terrier to join him.

The second job of the semicolon is worse. This is from an article about spas that I copyedited:

> "Now shower; and your skin will feel like silk," she told me.

Allow me to translate: "Look at me! I can use semicolons!"

This semicolon, used to separate two independent clauses, is perfectly legitimate. But independent clauses, by definition, can stand alone. So why wouldn't the writer let them do so? She could have used a comma. She could have made these two sentences. Or she could have used nothing.

Such semicolons are often justified, but they're never necessary—except for showing Readers that you know how to use them. It's the height of writer-serving writing and the root of my prejudice against semicolons.

I try to keep my prejudice in check. If I come across something like this, I leave it:

> Holly hadn't had a drink for weeks; she wanted one badly.

If the writer believes that these independent clauses are so closely linked that they belong in the same sentence, it's not my place as a copy editor to disagree. But when I'm the writer, I just separate the sentences.

Other, more reasonable experts also dislike semicolons: "The semicolon is an ugly bastard, and thus I tend to avoid it," writes *Washington Post* business copy desk chief Bill Walsh in the book *Lapsing Into a Comma*. That brings us to another important point: Readability and aesthetics go hand in hand. A sentence riddled with semicolons can be hard on the eyes—Readers' eyes.

"My advice to writers just starting out? Don't use semicolons!" Kurt Vonnegut said in a 2007 speech. "They are transvestite hermaphrodites, representing exactly nothing. All they do is suggest you might have gone to college."

Parentheses, on the other hand, can be indispensable. But often they can make a sentence messy and overly busy. And, like semicolons, they tend to get abused. Here's an example:

> CarCo's L9 Sports Activity Coupe claims to marry coupe-like handling to SUV-ish utility. Though it's more coupe (the fastest version does 0–60 mph in 5.3 seconds) than SUV (offering less cargo space than CarCo's smaller L4 crossover), the instantly recognizable L9 comes close to the hype.

An article writer's job is to make information easily digestible. But parentheses often amount to force-feeding. They tell the Reader,

"I couldn't be bothered weaving all the important facts into a readable narrative, so I just crammed them in here."

Yes, it's more work to craft the facts into palatable sentences, but that's the writer's job:

> CarCo's L9 Sports Activity Coupe claims to marry coupe-like handling with SUV-ish utility. It's more coupe than SUV. The fastest version does 0–60 mph in 5.3 seconds, and it offers less cargo space than CarCo's smaller L4 crossover. Yet the instantly recognizable L9 comes close to the hype.

Sometimes, parentheses really are the best way to serve the information to the Reader. Usually, the smaller the parenthetical insertion, the better it works. The more stuff crammed between the parentheses and the more parentheses crammed into the sentence, the bigger the clue that the sentence needs an overhaul.

If you disagree, you're in good company. Some writers love parentheses and use them to the delight of their Readers. David Foster Wallace was king of the envelope-pushing parentheses:

> The CNN sound tech (Mark A., 29, from Atlanta, and after Jay the tallest person on the Trail, vertiginous to talk to, able to get a stick's boom mike directly over McCain's head from the back of even the thickest scrum) has brought out from a complexly padded case a Sony SX-Series Portable Digital Editor ($32,000 retail) and connected it to some headphones and to Jonathan Karl's Dell Latitudes laptop and cell phone, and the three of them are running the CNN videotape of this morning's South Carolina Criminal Justice Academy address, trying to find a certain place where Jonathan Karl's notes

indicate that McCain said something like "Regardless of how Governor Bush and his surrogates have distorted my position on the death penalty . . ."

(And if you think a 38-word parenthetical insertion plus a 2-word parenthetical insertion in a 126-word sentence is astounding, you should see the guy's footnotes. But I parenthetically digress. . .)

This goes to show you how stupid prejudices are. Wallace was a prizewinning and critically acclaimed writer. So clearly, my small-minded view of parentheses doesn't apply. Still . . . how it burns in me.

Wallace used parentheses to create a maze of ideas—a place where Readers can meander and explore. His parentheticals were devices used for the benefit of the Reader and not for the convenience of the writer. Many loved them. Me, I can appreciate what Wallace was doing, but I'm not a fan of these parentheticals and footnotes. I like my information served linear—one bite at a time.

Parentheses can also be used as a sort of voice device—slipping in wry observations, ironies, exclamations, and other little bits of commentary:

George told me he was going out for a pack of cigarettes (yeah, right) and that I shouldn't wait up.

I have no problem with these parentheses. In fact, I like them. They create a nod or a wink or a whisper of "look out." They can add a layer of meaning or a caveat or humor. The difference to me is that, unlike the info-cramming parentheses that serve the writer, parentheses as a voice device serve the Reader.

You can form your own opinions about parentheses and semi-colons. Just remember who they're for.

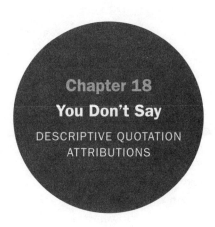

Chapter 18
You Don't Say
DESCRIPTIVE QUOTATION
ATTRIBUTIONS

I edit a writer who does this a lot:

> "The menu is all new," Jones enthused.

> "Schools in the area are improving," Principal Wilson
> enthused.

> "I'm enthused," I enthused.

Okay, maybe not that last one. But for all this writer's love of
enthused for quotation attributions, guess how many times I've left
it alone. Zero. Zippo. I change every single one. My justification is
that, technically, this is an incorrect use of the verb. Look it up in
a dictionary and you'll see that you can be enthused, you can even
enthuse *over* something, but you can't enthuse *something*. It's not a
transitive verb, at least not the way this writer uses it.

But that's just my excuse. The real reason is that I find *enthused*
annoying. In journalism circles, *said* is a virtue—simple, precise, and
unadorned—and alternatives to it are considered frilly and silly. You

don't have to agree, but be aware that lots of editors hold this view. Choose your alternatives to *said* with great care.

Fiction gives you a little more creative elbow room, but not carte blanche. *He hissed* sometimes works. *Screamed*, *hollered*, *moaned*, *explained*, and *replied* all work well in some attributions. A lot of editors don't mind *laughed* for quotation attribution. I leave that one alone, but others change it. I change *he extolled*, and I consider *echoed the sentiment* a red flag telling me that the writer is just stringing together quotations, which doesn't qualify as writing.

An attribution should tell the Reader who was speaking. If possible, it can also convey a bit more information, like emotion. But *said* shouldn't be thrown out just because the writer is hell-bent on flaunting her uniqueness or creativity.

Here's another problem that crops up a lot in descriptive quotation attributions:

> "Our redesigned casino will be better than ever," general manager and CEO Michael Roberts said, suggesting visitors try out the new higher-paying slot machines and the redesigned poker room while visiting the property and adding that the restaurant is now open 24 hours as well.

This goes back to our lesson on participles as modifiers. *Adding*, *suggesting*, *noting*, *implying*, *referring to*, and similar terms can all modify *said*, but some writers depend too much on this device. A quotation attribution is not an ideal place to squeeze in tons of extra information. When the result feels artificial, just make a new sentence or two.

"Our redesigned casino will be better than ever," general manager and CEO Michael Roberts said~~,.~~ ~~suggesting~~ <u>He suggested</u> visitors try out the new higher-paying slot machines and the redesigned poker room~~.~~ ~~while visiting the property and adding~~ <u>He added</u> that the restaurant is now open 24 hours ~~as well~~.

If you like to get creative with quotation attributions, do. But do so because it works, not because you want to show off or be different. When in doubt, remember that *said* is an old friend you can always fall back on.

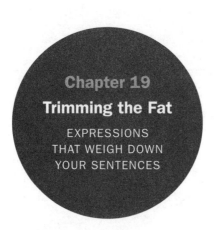

Chapter 19

Trimming the Fat

EXPRESSIONS
THAT WEIGH DOWN
YOUR SENTENCES

In *Reading Like a Writer,* Francine Prose excerpts the first sentence of Samuel Johnson's *The Life of Savage.* The sentence is 134 words long. But Prose, a veteran writing teacher, doesn't criticize Johnson's monster sentence. She praises it. Her reason: The sentence, Prose says, is "economical."

The term *economy of words* crops up a lot in newspaper editing. When you're cranking out a hundred thousand copies a day on none-too-cheap newsprint, you're no fan of wasted ink. So, for as long as papers are printed on paper, there will continue to be a startling correlation between "all the news that's fit to print" and "all the news that fits." But economy of words is no less a virtue in an online article or an eight-hundred-page saga about hobbits or alien overlords. Why, you ask? I'll give you a moment to answer your own question. That's right. Because of the Reader. His time is valuable, his attention span may be short, his opportunities for diversions are infinite, and his willingness to read your writing is a blessing for which you should be grateful.

Don't waste his time. Learn to root out flabby writing and to streamline sentences to make every word count.

There's a difference between fatty sentences and long sentences. Yes, they're often one and the same. But not always. A 134-word sentence can be tight and economical, while an 8-word sentence can contain 7 words of lard—or even 8.

Keeping the blubber out of your sentences is no easy feat. Fatty prose sneaks into writing in many ways. It can take the form of an unnecessary adverb, a ridiculous redundancy, a self-conscious over-explaining, a cliché, or jargon. You should develop the habit of always considering whether your sentence would be better if you chopped out or swapped out a word, phrase, or clause. Develop the habit of considering whether each sentence is itself an asset or a liability.

In this chapter, we'll look at the fatty sentence problems that are easiest to fix—the unnecessary words and verbose little insertions that so often plague writers. We'll also look at the scary-sounding but really quite simple concepts of run-on sentences and comma splices. We'll save the deeper structural problems for the next chapter.

Adjectives can contribute to fatty prose. Considering how indispensable they are, that's surprising. Yet, often, they're dead weight.

Take, for example, this much-maligned first sentence of *The Da Vinci Code*:

> Renowned curator Jacques Saunière staggered through the vaulted archway of the museum's Grand Gallery.

There are two adjectives in this sentence, not counting *Grand*, which is part of a proper name. One of our two adjectives is fine. The other is—I'm not the first to say it—terrible.

Vaulted is serviceable. Not good, not bad. It may help some Readers make a mental picture. To others it may add nothing to *archway*. But it's justified.

Renowned, however, stinks. And that's not just my opinion. Linguist Geoffrey Pullum has made the same observation: this *Da Vinci Code* sentence contains a classic example of an adjective trying to stand in for real information. Remember, this is the first sentence of the book, and already the author is telling us what to think about one of his characters and shirking his due diligence to show us *why* this character is renowned.

So what's the alternative to *The Da Vinci Code*'s approach? Let's look at some other writers' choices:

> In the late summer of 1922, my grandmother Desdemona
> Stephanides wasn't predicting births but deaths, specifically,
> her own.

In this passage from *Middlesex*, Jeffrey Eugenides doesn't say *my eccentric grandmother, my hypochondriac grandmother,* or *my neurotic grandmother*. Within a few sentences, it will become clear that she is all those things: "Desdemona became what she'd remain for the rest of her life: a sick person imprisoned in a healthy body." Eugenides didn't need to slap an adjective in front of *grandmother* to make his point.

Let's look at another example of an adjective that never was:

It's somewhere above Nebraska I remember I left my fish behind.

Chuck Palahniuk could have written *my beloved fish* or even *my beloved butterscotch-colored fish*. He didn't. He started chapter 39 of *Survivor* with that simple sentence, then waited awhile to add, "It's crazy, but you invest all your emotion in just this one tiny goldfish, even after six hundred and forty goldfish, and you can't just let the little thing starve to death." That's how we know that it's beloved and that it's gold.

In other words, perhaps the best way to fix our *Da Vinci Code* sentence is to get rid of the adjective *renowned* altogether—maybe even get rid of the modifying noun *curator* and the adjective *vaulted*—and wait for a better opportunity to convey the information. No doubt, that's what some more critically acclaimed writers would have done:

Jacques Saunière staggered through the archway of the museum's Grand Gallery.

Adjectives aren't bad. They can be wonderful, and as predicates they can work perfectly: *Frau Helga was **tall**.*

But adjectives are no substitute for solid information. Often they have that less-is-more thing working against them: *The big, terrifying, homicidal, totally out-of-control escaped convict ran toward me* does not achieve its desired effect. Better to just say, *The escaped convict ran toward me* and leave it at that.

If it helps, divide adjectives into two categories: facts and value judgments. Adjectives that express fact can be fine. But adjectives that impose value judgments on your Reader are trouble. *Bloodied and limping curator Jacques Saunière*, though awkward, is still better than *Awesome and brilliant curator Jacques Saunière*.

Worse, sometimes adjectives are meaningless. *The exact same* means *the same*. The only difference is that in *the exact same*, it's clear the writer is trying to pound home her point. As we know, this can backfire, weakening the point.

If all this talk about adjectives reminds you of our adverbs chapter, there's a good reason for that. Adjectives and adverbs carry the same risks. Here's an example:

> The freshly rejuvenated $70-million Sands Resort & Spa
> hearkens to Vegas's glory days.

Unless you're actively trying to root out wasteful words, you might not notice that the word *freshly* modifying *rejuvenated* is about as meaningful as *freshly refreshed*. Pure redundancy.

Look at the sentence without the goldbricking adverb:

> The rejuvenated $70-million Sands Resort & Spa hearkens to
> Vegas's glory days.

The *freshly* had a brain-numbing effect, as if the writer used it just to meet a word count minimum. The streamlined version, though just one word shorter, emphasizes substance. It has more power to command the Reader's attention.

As we saw in chapter 7, manner adverbs can backfire, making an idea seem weak even as it struggles to make it strong. But adverbs can also create redundancies: *already existing, previously done, first begin, currently working*.

Of course, adverbs need not be redundant to be flabby:

> Sarah quickly grabbed a knife.

> Sarah grabbed a knife.

Does *quickly* really add anything to the sentence? Or does the less-is-more principle render the second sentence better? Some may disagree, and there may be times when *quickly* adds a crucial bit of information. But to me this sentence better conveys immediacy without the word *quickly*.

Watch out for manner adverbs that add no solid information: *extremely, very, really, incredibly, unbelievably, astonishingly, totally, truly, currently, presently, formerly, previously.*

Also watch out for ones that try too hard to add impact to actions: *cruelly, happily, wantonly, angrily, sexily, alluringly, menacingly, blissfully.*

All these words have their place. They appear in the best writing, but more often they're found in the worst writing. So consider them red flags and weigh their use carefully.

Adverbs and adjectives aren't the only flabby accessories that show up in writing. Here's an example modeled after a real sentence I came across in my copyediting work:

> In addition to on-the-clock volunteer opportunities, ABC Co.
> also offers standard healthcare benefits, adoption assistance
> and flexible scheduling to help employees cultivate work/life
> balance.

I hate *in addition to*. Don't get me wrong, I write it all the time. And only about half the time do I remember that Writer June is doing something Reader June can't stand. But just because I'm guilty of this one doesn't mean I have much sympathy for the writer who throws an unnecessary *in addition to* my way.

Not every *in addition to* is bad. Sometimes it's a valid choice. But usually, *in addition to* refers to something that's already been discussed at length. In our sample sentence, it's clear that the reader already knows something about the on-the-clock volunteer opportunities being discussed. Chances are that the writer just finished discussing them and was looking for a segue to the next topic. In other words, she was saying, "In addition to the stuff I just told you about, here's another thing."

You can achieve the same effect by saying, *Here's another thing.* Or better yet, just get to the other thing.

This brings us to another problem with our original sentence: The *in addition to* phrase introduces a clause that contains the word *also.* This is a redundancy. It renders the entire *in addition to* phrase a complete waste. The writer should have simply said,

> ABC Co. also offers standard healthcare benefits, adoption assistance and flexible scheduling to help employees cultivate work/life balance.

We could also ask, Do we need to say *to help employees cultivate work/life balance*? The answer is more subjective, but it's worth considering whether we should chop it out.

There are a lot of other little phrases that, like *in addition to*, can be pure fat. In the original *Elements of Style*, William Strunk Jr. told his Cornell students, "Omit needless words," then went on to list examples. "The question as to whether," Strunk wrote, can be just "whether." "Used for fuel purposes" can be "used for fuel." "This is a subject which" can be just "this subject."

Strunk was especially emphatic with his students about *the fact that*: "The expression *the fact that* should be revised out of every sentence in which it occurs."

The Elements of Style was not written as a book of universal writing laws. It was a classroom style guide for Strunk's Cornell students. So you can discard any advice in it you don't agree with. But there's some wisdom you can use here. Consider whether these expressions are indeed needless, and if so, delete them.

I'm more liberal on *the fact that*. Sometimes it's the best way to show that an abstract concept is functioning as a noun:

That Robbie steals means he's a thief.

The fact that Robbie steals means he's a thief.

Because *the fact* is a noun phrase, it's more easily recognized as a subject than the subordinate clause *that Robbie steals*. Still, there's wisdom in the traditional caveat. *The fact that* is often pure lard. Use it as a measure of last resort after you've considered recasting the sentence:

Because Robbie steals, he's a thief.

I'm more conservative on *due to the fact that*. That's just a tedious way of saying *because*.

Other flabby figures of speech to watch out for include *in terms of, for his part, he is a man who, the exact same, taking into account, as if this weren't enough, considering all that*—the list goes on.

141

He is a man who and other terms with this structure are especially troubling: *It is a place that, dancing is an activity that, John's is a house that, cooking is a thing that.* They all follow the form

> noun/pronoun + to be + noun/pronoun that refers to the same thing as first + relative pronoun

This structure shifts the focus away from the important stuff by dedicating the main clause to ridiculously obvious information:

> *He is a man* who works very hard.

> *Paris is a place* that gets snow.

> *Dancing is an activity* that amounts to good exercise.

> *John's (house) is a house* that was built in the 1800s.

In all these sentences, the new information is trapped in the relative clause—those clauses that begin with *that, which, who,* or *whom* and that we learned about in chapter 8. The main clause is devoid of new information. It has the same problem as the upside-down subordination we covered in chapter 2 because the most interesting information isn't getting top billing in the sentence.

To fix a sentence with this structure, just make the new information your main clause:

HOLLOW MAIN CLAUSE	INFORMATIVE MAIN CLAUSE
He is a man who works very hard.	He works very hard.
Paris is a place that gets snow.	Paris gets snow.
Dancing is an activity that amounts to good exercise.	Dancing is good exercise.
John's is a house that was built in the 1800s.	John's house was built in the 1800s.

Keep your eyes peeled for this construction and be prepared to correct it.

Here's another term that is often a waste of ink: *for his part*. You'd think it would be rare. But I've seen it quite a few times in my copyediting work. This is a slight alteration of a real sentence I copyedited:

> For Brady's part, as the director of the Center for Computer Security at the Information Institute at the university, emphasis is on training students for the programming path.

This sentence has a number of problems, but none so glaring or so easily fixed as *for Brady's part*. *For Brady* says the same thing with fewer words. In fact, I can't think of a situation in which *for so-and-so's part* is better than just *for so-and-so*.

And here's an oddball little construction that crops up a lot in feature writing: *from blank to blank*. There's nothing wrong with *from . . . to* constructions, so it astounds me that they're so often the culprit in bad sentences. Here are some examples I've run across in my copyediting work:

> Everything from what software will be needed to how someone will book a trip and pay needs to be developed for the business.

> From donating a few hours weekly to nearby hospitals to par-
> ticipating in breast or ovarian cancer walks to raise research
> funds, millions of us donate our time and skills to myriad orga-
> nizations and causes.

And here's one with a double whammy of *in addition to* and *from
. . . to*:

> In addition to being the epicenter of bridal up-dos for those
> getting married on the expansive lawns, the Alex Remo Salon
> also caters to stressed-out guests with a comprehensive
> menu of facials, which range from the Moisturizing Hydration
> Facial, which utilizes protein, essential oils and active
> serums to relieve dry and sensitive skin; to the Star Facial,
> a 75-minute microdermabrasion session that reduces the
> appearance of scars, fine lines and wrinkles.

Yep. Those are all real sentences with a few names changed to
protect the innocent. (Didn't believe me when I told you that *from
. . . to* constructions are a common problem in feature writing, did
you?)

A *from . . . to* construction can set up a very long introductory
phrase. The main clause has to wait until the *from . . . to* observation
is complete, which can take a while.

No matter how long, a *from blank to bank* construction usually
works as a modifier. It's not hard to understand why an eight-, ten-,
or twenty-word modifier can be cumbersome.

My best advice here is don't rely on this construction too much
and be prepared to abandon it if it starts to get unwieldy. If your
from or your *to* contains its own *from* or *to*, you're probably making

a mess, as we saw previously in **to** *participating in breast or ovarian cancer walks* **to** *raise research funds*. If it requires semicolons to hold it all together, maybe you should recast the sentence.

Also, remember that there's no comma between the *from* and the *to*:

> From soup to nuts.

That's easy to see in short *from . . . to* phrases. But longer ones get confusing, inviting errant commas:

> From soup made with the finest ingredients from age-old recipes, to chocolate-covered nuts we hand dip, to the moment when you get the check, you'll love our service.

The first two commas shouldn't be there. Remember: *from blank to blank to blank* is comma free even when your blanks are so long that they make you forget you were using this construction in the first place. Of course, that's probably a sign that your *from . . . to* setup isn't cutting it.

Fatty prose can also happen because a writer is reluctant to make a bold statement:

> Hawaiians have adopted a lifestyle that is decidedly more leisurely and tolerant than that of their fellows on the mainland.

This problem crops up a lot in my own writing. But editing others' writing is helping. I'm learning that it's worth the effort to look for bold alternatives:

> The Hawaiian lifestyle is leisurely and tolerant.

Open up a copy of the *New York Times* or the *Washington Post* and you'll see lots of sentences like the latter example but almost none like the former. That's because top publications hate mealy-mouthed allusions and love solid, information-packed statements. I try to remember that.

Another example of fatty prose, again based on a real sentence by a professional writer:

> One of the more remarkable aspects of the park is the fact
> that it has eight manicured gardens.

Compare that to the alternative:

> The park has eight manicured gardens.

These six words do a better job of conveying the information than do the eighteen words in the first sentence. You get extra points if you noticed that, in the first example, the most notable information was crammed into a subordinate clause and used *the fact that*.

Don't underestimate the Reader. He can decide for himself whether having eight manicured gardens qualifies as *remarkable*. You're wasting his time by saying it's an *aspect* of the park. The Reader can connect one idea to the next without the help of *in addition to*. And he understands that *the Hawaiian lifestyle is leisurely and tolerant* is a generalization and subject to debate—no disclaimers required.

In other words, fatty insertions that can seem so meaningful when we're writing are often unnecessary at best and insufferable at worst. When in doubt, take them out.

Redundancies can be hard to spot. Vigilance is your best defense. Consider this sentence:

Flu viruses are known to be notoriously unpredictable.

We've seen how manner adverbs can create redundancies. But in this sentence, which I found in a *Los Angeles Times* article, the adverb isn't the problem.

Notoriously, by definition, means that something is well-known. Therefore, it's redundant with *are known*. But this adverb is pulling its weight and then some. It tells us in a single word that flu viruses *are known* for something. But because its definition also carries a negative connotation, *notoriously* adds extra information. The unpredictability of flu viruses isn't just famous, it's famously bad. That's why I suspect that, with a little more time or coffee, the copyeditor would have chopped out *known to be*, leaving just

Flu viruses are notoriously unpredictable.

Keep an eye out for these redundancies. Your ability to catch them will improve with practice.

Oh, and about those demons known as run-on sentences and comma splices: don't let the jargon intimidate you. You've already mastered far tougher concepts. Just note, for the record, a run-on sentence fails to properly link its clauses:

Elephants are large they eat foliage.

A comma splice, really just a type of run-on sentence, uses commas to link clauses that should stand on their own as sentences or at least be separated with a semicolon or conjunction:

Elephants are large, they eat foliage.

Both are easy to fix. Either make each clause a separate sentence, find some conjunction that can get the job done, or consider a semicolon:

Elephants are large. They eat foliage.

Elephants are large; they eat foliage.

Elephants are large, and they eat foliage.

Elephants are large because they eat foliage.

To fix flabby writing, watch out for words or little clusters of words that work well in speech but that don't translate well to the written word. Consider first whether you can cut them out altogether. If not, look for ways to streamline: *In addition to the fact that tuition is affordable* might be replaced with just *also*. Some fatty insertions can be cut altogether. *For his part, as director for the Center for Computer Security, Brady emphasizes training* says no less if you chop out *for his part*.

Also, watch out for sentences too cowardly to come out and say something or whose wording is just too convoluted. Remember that your goal is not fewer words, but economy of words.

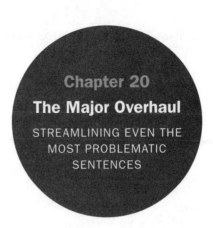

In previous chapters, we've seen some simple ways to pare down inefficient sentences. But some sentences have deeper structural problems that are harder to identify and harder to fix. Luckily, you now have enough grammar under your belt to tackle any problem that can muck up a sentence.

Whenever you're faced with a problem sentence, start by looking for its main clause—that is, its main subject and verb:

> This intimate and discerning depiction of the impact of migration on families left behind by loved ones who travel north emerges as a nuanced portrait of "the other side" of the immigration story.

This is a description of a movie in a film festival. Movie loglines are tough to write because they're supposed to be kept to just one or two sentences. But this sentence appeared in a brochure—not in a pitch to a Hollywood executive. So the writer had the elbow room to improve it. The question, of course, is how?

Start by isolating the main subject, *depiction*, and verb, *emerges*. So, at its heart, our sentence is

This depiction emerges.

That's a complete sentence. But is it a complete thought? Does it tell the Reader what to expect from this movie? Not even close. Clearly, we need some of that other stuff. For example, *depiction*, on its own, is painfully devoid of any solid information. Also, a depiction is always a depiction *of* something. That's where the trouble began for the writer. A prepositional phrase—an *of* phrase—was needed just to make sense of the subject.

Then there's *emerges*. This is an intransitive verb, so it doesn't need an object. But it sure needs something. Hence the *as* that follows. This *as* creates a vehicle to help tell the Reader what, exactly, *depiction* is doing in this sentence. The depiction is not just emerging—coming out of a hole or coming into the spotlight. It's emerging *as* something. We can presume that by *emerging as*, the writer means "reveals itself to be" or "comes to be" or "turns out to be" or "becomes." In other words, *emerges as* is the writer's substitute for *is*. Yes, it's more creative than *is*, but that creativity comes at too high a price. We already have a subject that needs a prepositional phrase to make sense. Now we're using a verb that also needs a prepositional phrase to make sense. (Note: *As* is often a conjunction. But in our sentence it's a preposition. We know this because subordinating conjunctions like *as* introduce whole clauses but prepositions take objects—nouns or pronouns, like *portrait*.)

To mean anything at all, our main clause must be expanded to

> This depiction *of the impact of migration* emerges *as a nuanced portrait.*

Impact is the object of a preposition in a prepositional phrase. Then *impact* is followed by its own prepositional phrase, *of migration*, yet *impact* is still begging for yet another prepositional phrase. Impacts are usually impacts *on* someone or something. Hence *on families* in the writer's original:

> of the impact of migration on families

What families? Well, we have a modifier to answer that. It's the participial phrase *left behind*. But that modifier requires a prepositional phrase, *by loved ones*. And *loved ones*, the object of the preposition *by*, takes as a modifier the relative clause *who travel north*. Each of the modifying phrases and clauses is underlined here:

> This depiction <u>of the impact</u> <u>of migration</u> <u>on families</u> <u>left behind</u> <u>by loved ones</u> <u>who travel north</u>

All that comes before we even get to the verb.

Then, after the verb *emerges*, which requires its own prepositional phrase, *as a portrait*, we still need two more prepositional phrases: *of "the other side"* and *of the immigration story*:

> emerges <u>as a portrait</u> <u>of "the other side"</u> <u>of the immigration story</u>

After all that, the writer squeezed in three adjectives: *intimate* and *discerning* before *depiction* and *nuanced* before *portrait*.

Sift through all the clutter in this sentence and you find that the very heart—the very point of our main clause—is

This depiction is a portrait.

That's a whole lotta nuthin'. It's like saying this picture is an image, this person is a man, or this car is a vehicle. A total waste of words that, ironically, happened in a place where economy of words was paramount. The main clause contained no new information. The substantive stuff was all crammed into prepositional phrases and other sentence accessories.

Despite all these problems, the writer did a pretty impressive job of getting the point across. We know what the film is about and we even get a sense of mood. But how could we do better?

Well, our main clause contains both a troublesome noun and a troublesome verb. Let's try replacing them. Whenever you're struggling with a vague or troublesome noun, first consider the simplest alternatives. Ask yourself, what is this thing we're talking about? *This depiction* referred to a film. *Emerges* really referred to a state of being. Simplify them and you get

This ~~depiction~~ film ~~emerges as~~ is

I still don't like our verb. Yes, it's a simpler alternative to *emerges as*. But *is* sets up something self-evident, like *this film is a film*. Is there any more interesting action we could convey with our verb? Yes.

This film depicts.

Now we have a more tangible (if more pedestrian) subject and a more action-oriented verb. If we drop this into the first part of our sentence, we end up with something like this:

> This intimate and discerning film depicts the impact of migration on families left behind by loved ones who travel north.

But we have this left over from the original:

> a nuanced portrait of "the other side" of the immigration story

What can we do with this leftover information? We could tack it on:

> This intimate and discerning film depicts the impact of migration on families left behind by loved ones who travel north—a nuanced portrait of "the other side" of the immigration story.

Not bad. But the crux of our sentence is now

> This film depicts the impact *and* is a portrait.

So we're still making the hollow statement *this film is a portrait.* We could break our sentence into two, thereby giving *portrait* a real job to do:

> This intimate and discerning film depicts the impact of migration on families left behind by loved ones who travel north. It is a nuanced portrait of "the other side" of the immigration story.

Or we could use the coordinator *and* and another verb like *forms* to keep everything in a single sentence:

> This intimate and discerning film depicts the impact of migration on families left behind by loved ones who travel north *and forms* a nuanced portrait of "the other side" of the immigration story.

Or better yet we could avoid the redundancy of *this film forms a portrait* by making *portrait* our main subject:

> This intimate, discerning, and nuanced *portrait* of "the other side" of the immigration story depicts the impact on families left behind by loved ones who travel north.

Now we can see that we sure did have a lot of adjectives offering commentary on this film. Maybe we can do without one. For example, *discerning* surely meant something important to the writer. But it doesn't mean much to a Reader. If we're voting one of them off the island, that would be my pick:

> This intimate and nuanced portrait of "the other side" of the immigration story depicts the impact on families left behind by loved ones who travel north.

We might even ditch another adjective:

> This intimate portrait of "the other side" of the immigration story depicts the impact on families left behind by loved ones who travel north.

I like this much better. It still has stacked modifiers—four prepositional phrases and a relative clause. It still has *impact on*. But these no longer seem like problems because the noise around them has been silenced.

And this isn't the only alternative. Your grammar skills open up a world of choices:

> By looking at the families left behind when loved ones travel north, this intimate and discerning film shows the other side of the immigration story.

> *Film Name Unknown* is an intimate portrait of the families whose loved ones move north to find work.

> We've all heard the stories of Mexican nationals who travel north to find work. But what about the families they leave behind? The intimate and nuanced *Film Name Unknown* tells their stories.

> When Jose left Guatemala to find work in the United States, he did it for his family. Little did he know the ripple effect that his absence would create.

Some of these examples wouldn't work. The last two especially don't have the tone of film festival movie descriptions. But these examples help us see the wide range of possibilities that open up once we get to the heart of a sentence and consider what, exactly, we're trying to say.

Let's look at another sentence:

> The United States government's plan to rid banks of lethal assets has precious metals investors speculating that the economy and lending groups may be reviving.

Our subject is *plan*. Our verb is *has*. The object of our verb is *investors* followed by the modifier *speculating*. Remember from chapter 10 that participles can work as modifiers.

Any sentence built on a foundation of *has + noun or pronoun + present participle* stuffs the action into a participial phrase or clause: *The plan has them speculating.* To make *speculating* a real action, you'd have to rejigger the whole sentence:

> Since the government announced plans to rid banks of lethal assets, precious metals investors *are speculating* that the economy and lending groups may be reviving.

> The government plans to rid banks of lethal assets. So precious metals investors *are speculating* that the economy and lending groups may be reviving.

> Precious metals investors *are speculating* that the economy and lending groups may be reviving. Why? Because the government plans to rid banks of lethal assets.

In all of these, we made *speculating* an action instead of a modifier. In the last two examples, we changed the noun *plans* into the verb *plans*—extracting another action out of our original sentence.

Here's a longer passage. It's modeled after a real excerpt from an article I edited:

> Sky diving. Rock climbing. River rafting. Guess which one is the odd man out in the emerging world of new vacation choices for an aging population that, increasingly, is more active and healthy and less willing to follow their parents'

footsteps when it comes to choosing how to live out their golden years. The answer: They all belong in the mix, according to gerontology experts.

The fourth sentence is extremely problematic. It's too busy, but that's not the worst of it. The whole sentence teeters on the idea that the Reader is supposed to *guess which one* of the listed items is *the odd man out.* What's the reward for the Reader who takes up the challenge? He learns that there is no *odd man out.* They all belong in the mix. It's as if the Cookie Monster on Sesame Street had sung his "One of These Things Is Not Like the Other" song in front of identical plates of cookies.

The very point of the fourth sentence had to go. Here's how the passage looked after I edited it:

> Skydiving. Rock climbing. River rafting. They're not exactly hallmarks of senior recreation. But a new generation of seniors is changing that. Healthier and more adventurous than the generations of retirees before them, today's seniors are making some surprising choices about how to spend their golden years.

Here's another problem sentence. It uses a clause in place of a noun phrase and another clause as a modifier:

> That you work so hard is the reason that you're getting a raise.

Fix it by looking for ways to get the action unstuck:

> You work hard. So you're getting a raise.

Here's good exercise. Find the problem in the following sentence:

> Working in both the feature film and television worlds, Radoff
> Entertainment develops material for both the big and small
> screens.

You'd be amazed how often I see sentences like this. In fact, this is a disguised version of a real sentence I copyedited. The clauses are redundant. Notice how much better the sentence is chopped in half:

> Radoff Entertainment develops feature films and television
> programs.

Here's a sentence that you should now know how to improve:

> Another activity at the Family Fun Center is the opportunity for
> kids to create a journal.

This has that *a blank is a blank* structure as its main clause, stating little more than *an activity is an opportunity.* You'd do better to make the main verb a real action:

> Kids at the Family Fun Center can also create a journal.

Now that you're getting good at this, we can look at a longer piece. Here's a thinly disguised rewrite of an unpublished story by an amateur writer. As you read it, keep an eye out for words, phrases, and even whole sentences that should go:

> I have done something everyone knows you shouldn't do—
> that being I fell for a @!#$ friend.
>
> Slowly over a period of just a few weeks I fell in love with
> him. I couldn't help myself even though I had known that it

was a stupid thing to do and that such actions always have consequences. Now it appears I have just two choices. The first option is the most logical one; I should dump him and sever all contact before I fall even more deeply in love with him. The second option is to try to make a relationship that is serious and exclusive, but I have a feeling that that won't pan out. We're two different people. So of course I have selected none of these choices and simply continue sleeping with him.

Slowly turning the knob on a Sunday morning, I opened the door to Joe's apartment and peered inside. Joe was seated at his desk with a paintbrush in hand and he dabbed at a paint palette lying on a wooden chair beside him.

No doubt, the writer figured that every one of these words was needed. But the writer was wrong. The passage is teeming with unnecessary and obvious statements, flabby prose, and wasteful redundancies. If I were editing this story, here's what I would do to it:

I ~~have done something everyone knows you shouldn't do—that being~~ did something stupid. I fell for a @!#$ friend. ~~Slowly over a period of just a few weeks I fell in love with him.~~ I couldn't help myself. ~~even though I had known that it was a stupid thing to do and that such actions always have consequences. Now it appears I have just two choices. The first option is the most logical one;~~ I suppose I should dump Joe ~~him and sever all contact~~ before I fall even more deeply in love ~~with him. The second option is to~~ Or I could try to make it a serious relationship ~~that is serious and exclusive~~, but I have a feeling that that wouldn't pan out. ~~We're two different~~

159

> ~~people.~~ So ~~of course I~~ ~~have selected none of these choices~~ ~~and simply~~ just continue sleeping with him.
>
> ~~Slowly turning the knob o~~On a Sunday morning, I opened the door to Joe's apartment ~~and peered inside~~. Joe was seated at his desk ~~with~~ dabbing a paintbrush ~~in hand and he~~ ~~dabbed~~ at a ~~paint~~ palette ~~lying~~ on a wooden chair beside him.

Let's take a closer look at these edits:

> I ~~have done something everyone knows you shouldn't do—~~ ~~that being~~ did something stupid. I fell for a ~~@!#$~~ friend.

The first sentence was too wordy. *That being* is especially flabby and unprofessional. So I chopped. Perhaps the word *stupid* doesn't capture what the writer wanted to say. That's why I'd run all these changes by her. But, be it *stupid* or *wrong* or *moronic* or *unwise* or *shortsighted* or *childish*, somewhere out there is a word that will say what she means in fewer than six words.

In the original story, *@!#$* actually appeared in front of the noun. Bad choice. For one thing, if you're going to swear, fucking swear already. But, more important, any swear word here—explicit or candy coated—enfeebles the information. *I fell for a friend* has a power all its own. The writer's attempt to add oomph actually weakened her point.

> I couldn't help myself. ~~even though I had known that it was~~ ~~a stupid thing to do and that such actions always have~~ ~~consequences.~~

I couldn't help myself shows that the protagonist was conflicted. The rest just flogs the obvious.

> ~~Now it appears I have just two choices. The first option is the most logical one;~~

When you lay out two options, there's no need to first insert a sentence *saying* that you're about to lay out two options. Also, after the writer said she was about to lay out two options, she dedicated a whole sentence to evaluating one of the options she had yet to lay out. Whenever you find yourself buried under so many words, start by asking: can't I just chop all this out? The answer is usually yes.

> I suppose I should dump Joe ~~him and sever all contact~~ before I fall even more deeply in love ~~with him~~.

I should dump him, all by itself, makes it clear that she has options and which one she believes is best. Neither of the two preceding sentences was needed at all. They hurt the passage.

As for *I should dump him and sever all contact*: Why not dump him *and* sever all contact *and* change your phone number *and* avoid eye contact with anyone who has his hair color *and* burn every photo you have of him *and* tell him his mama's a tramp *and* try to get on with your life *and* call that cute barista at your local Starbucks? In other words, was it really necessary to dump him *and sever all contact*? Isn't there a single action—say, *dumping*—that could cover all the necessary bases here? Perhaps not, but probably.

> ~~The second option is to~~ Or I could try to make it a serious relationship ~~that is serious and exclusive~~, but I have a feeling that that wouldn't pan out.

Either *a serious relationship* or *an exclusive relationship* says enough. Even *a serious, exclusive relationship* is better than *a relationship that is serious and exclusive.*

> ~~We're two different people.~~

As worded, this is meaningless. Show me any two people and I'll show you two different people. But even if the writer had found a more logical way to make her point, perhaps with *we're too different,* this would raise questions she's not answering. If the protagonist suspects the relationship won't pan out, it's clear she has her reasons. To say it's because they're *two different people* or even *too different* is a tease. It's better to leave some stuff unexplained than to waste the Reader's time with half an answer or by telling him something he already knew: that people are different.

On the other hand, the writer could have said, "We're too different. I eat veal topped with foie gras, and he's a member of People for the Ethical Treatment of Lima Beans."

The point is, either explain or don't. But don't half-ass it.

> So ~~of course~~ I ~~have selected none of these choices and simply~~ just continue sleeping with him.

There were a lot of unnecessary words here. *I just continue sleeping with him* makes it clear that she rejected the dump-him option and the get-serious option.

> ~~Slowly turning the knob o~~On a Sunday morning, I opened the door to Joe's apartment ~~and peered inside~~.

I think I speak for Readers everywhere when I say we're familiar with the mechanics of door opening. No strangers to knob turning are we. So unless *how* she opened the door was important or interesting or entertaining, spare us the details. You could cut that down even more if you wanted to: *On a Sunday morning, I walked into Joe's apartment to find him sitting at his desk.* In fact, the act of entering may not be relevant at all: *On a Sunday morning, Joe was seated at his desk.* It's up to you. Just never fall victim to the idea that every little action in your story is critical. It's not.

> Joe was seated at his desk ~~with~~ <u>dabbing</u> a paintbrush ~~in hand and he dabbed~~ at a ~~paint~~ palette ~~lying~~ on a wooden chair beside him.

If you have a character who's dabbing a paintbrush into the colors on a palette, is it really worth the words to say the paintbrush is *in hand*? Ninety-nine times out of a hundred, no, it's not.

Of course, none of this is law. Skilled writers can defy all these principles effectively and with grace. But novice writers need to understand the concepts here. Flabby prose, repetitiveness, and statements beleaguering the obvious separate the amateurs from the pros. Make it a habit to seek out such lard in your own writing and start to look for ways in which chopping up or chopping out problem sentences can improve a whole work.

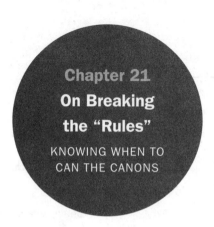

One theme has cropped up time and again in this book. You've probably noticed it. From the chapter on adverbs to my rant on parentheses, from the long Ian McEwan sentence to the even longer Cormac McCarthy sentence, we've seen over and over that writing rules are made to be broken. That is, they're not really rules at all. They're just baby steps we can take before we learn how to walk then run then jitterbug. They help us when we're struggling. But they need not weigh us down when we're soaring.

People argue about writing rules. For every teacher who tells you, "Omit needless words," another will tell you that's nonsense, citing examples of top-notch writers whose work teems with "needless words." For every peer who tells you, "Avoid adverbs," someone else will argue that manner adverbs are used extensively by many of the very best writers. For everyone who tells you to use short sentences or avoid the passive voice, someone else will argue that long sentences can be great and the passive can be an ideal choice.

Don't get entangled in these debates. Just understand the wisdom of both sides. Every one of the writing "rules" you hear is rooted in a good idea with at least some practical application. Yet none of these rules is worth a damn when stretched into an absolute. "Avoid manner adverbs" can be helpful advice for some writers and is worth noting by all writers—even those who disagree. But it's not law. The advice "Keep sentences short" can be just what the doctor ordered for less experienced writers prone to cumbersome sentences. But, clearly, it's not a real rule.

All the so-called rules are really just guidelines that can help you serve your Reader—or not. If they help you, use them. If not, disregard them entirely. You'll be in good company.

But remember: These guidelines are always there to fall back on if you get a little lost. Think of them not as rules but as safe havens. If you're getting into trouble with a long sentence, you can chop it into shorter sentences. If your adverb-laden sentence falls flat, you can just ditch the adverbs.

You're not bound by these rules. But you are subject to expectations. Depending on the Reader, the publication, the subject matter, the genre, the context, and the cachet of your byline, Readers may receive your work in different ways. Readers can have prejudices—some far more important than the rantings of a lone anti-semicolonite. A Reader who encounters a very long sentence in the *Palookaville Post* or in an unpublished manuscript by a new author may label it bad writing. But the Reader might consider the same sentence genius in anything with the name Philip Roth on the cover.

Perhaps that's unfair. Perhaps not. Maybe it means that Readers expect us to earn their respect before they'll give us the benefit of the doubt. Perhaps abstract painters have to deal with the same thing—they must prove they can draw a bowl of grapes before people will admire their abstract shapes or spatters. Maybe everyone deals with this stuff: stockbrokers and fashion designers and academics—everyone.

If Readers have prejudices, that's the writing world we live in. We must decide how to navigate it. We can't please all the Readers all the time and we shouldn't try. But we don't get to create our Readers in our own image, either. We don't get to tell them what to value or enjoy. We can write in a way true to our own voice and our own ideas of beauty and substance, and we can hope that some Readers appreciate it. But, even when we aim to serve the narrowest cross section of Readers, we're still working for the Readers we have. We should be grateful that we have them.

Thanks for listening.

Appendix 1

Grammar for Writers

:::::

To know grammar, focus on the parts of speech and how phrases and clauses form sentences. All that stuff you've heard about how you supposedly can't use *healthy* to mean *healthful* and how it's supposedly wrong to say "Can I be excused?" in place of "May I be excused?"—that's not grammar. That's usage (much of it pure lies). Further, all that perplexing stuff like whether to write out numbers or use numerals and whether to put a comma before an *and*—that's called style. One doesn't know usage or style. Like the most skilled editors, you must look these things up.

For usage matters, have a trusted dictionary such as a recent *American Heritage* or *Webster's New World* or *Merriam-Webster's Collegiate* and a good usage guide such as *Garner's Modern American Usage* or *Fowler's Modern English Usage* and look up issues as they arise. For style matters, book authors and most magazine writers should have a copy of *The Chicago Manual of Style.* Journalists and public relations professionals should have *The Associated Press Stylebook.* Organizations such as the Modern Language Association, the American Medical Association, and the American Psychological

Association have their own stylebooks. Usually, a professor or an employer will tell you if you need to follow one of these.

The nitpicky stuff—little matters of usage and style—can be looked up. But the stuff that will really help your writing is the mechanical, analytical stuff we call grammar. Throughout this book, we've touched on a lot of aspects of grammar. Here, now, is grammar long form.

Most grammar primers start with the parts of speech before moving on to phrases and clauses and then finally to sentence formation. But because we're most concerned with sentence formation, we'll reverse that order, looking first at sentence formation before moving on to phrase and clause structure and finally to the parts of speech, including how to form plurals of nouns and how to conjugate verbs.

Read or skim through this at least once. Then return to it whenever you need to better understand the mechanics of sentence writing.

Sentence Formation

There are five basic structures for simple sentences, which are sentences that contain just one clause. On top of these five structures, optional elements called adverbials can be added. The following table shows the basic structures.

STRUCTURE	EXAMPLE
Subject + verb	Phil knows.
Subject + transitive verb + direct object	Spiders trap flies.
Subject + transitive verb + indirect object + direct object	Sean gave Tim money.
Subject + copular verb + complement of the copular verb	Soda is sweet.
Subject + transitive verb + direct object + object complement	The voters elected Jones mayor.

An indirect object is in essence a prepositional phrase that comes before the direct object and that, in its new position, no longer requires the preposition:

> Robbie made spaghetti for his mother. [*His mother* is the object of the preposition *for.*]

> Robbie made his mother spaghetti. [*His mother* is an indirect object and is placed before the direct object *spaghetti*; the preposition *for* is omitted.]

> Jake sends love letters to Mary. [*Mary* is the object of the preposition *to.*]

> Jake sends Mary love letters. [*Mary* is an indirect object and is placed before the direct object *love letters*; the preposition *to* is omitted.]

A complement of a copular verb is not the same as an object of a transitive verb. An object receives the action of the verb, but the complement of a copular verb refers back to the subject:

> Anna seems *nice*.
>
> Boys become *men*.
>
> Coffee smells *good*.

An object of a transitive verb can have its own modifying complement. This is called an object complement (or an object predicative). The object complement can be an adjective phrase or a noun phrase. It describes the object or tells what the object has become:

> Spinach makes Pete *strong*. [The adjective *strong* is a complement of the object *Pete*.]
>
> Spinach makes Pete *a man*. [The noun phrase *a man* is a complement of the object *Pete*.]

A sentence with more than one independent clause is a compound sentence. In a compound sentence, the clauses can be coordinated with a coordinating conjunction. Coordinate clauses have equal grammatical status.

A sentence that contains at least one subordinate clause is called a complex sentence:

> Birds make nests and they sing. [compound sentence containing two coordinated clauses of equal grammatical weight]
>
> Because Andy is hungry, he eats. [complex sentence containing a subordinate clause and a main clause]

Subjects and objects can be phrases or whole clauses:

> The dog sees that you are scared [The subject is the noun phrase *the dog*; the object of the verb *sees* is the subordinate clause *that you are scared.*]

> To know him is to love him [*To know* is an infinitive clause functioning as the subject of the verb *is*; *to love* is an infinitive clause functioning as a complement of the verb.]

ADVERBIALS

Other sentence elements, called adverbials, can be added on to the basic sentence structures. An adverbial can be an adverb, a prepositional phrase, a clause, or a noun phrase. Though an adverbial may contain crucial information, it is not crucial to the sentence's core structure in the way that subjects, verbs, objects, and complements are.

For example, in *The van followed Harry to the park*, remove the adverbial (the prepositional phrase *to the park*) and you retain a grammatical sentence: *The van followed Harry*. Like adverbs, adverbials can answer the questions when, where, in what manner, and to what degree, or they can modify whole sentences. Or, like adjectives, they can modify nouns. The following examples illustrate adverbials:

> The van followed Harry *to the park.* [prepositional phrase answering the question *where*]

> The van followed Harry *this afternoon.* [noun phrase answering the question *when*]

> *In addition*, the van followed Harry. [prepositional phrase connecting the sentence to a prior thought]

The van *discreetly* followed Harry. [adverb modifying the verb *followed*]

The van followed Harry *where he walked.* [whole clause answering the question where]

NEGATION

Sentences are said to be positive or negative. Sentences can be made negative by inserting *not* after the operator, which is usually the first word in the verb phrase but can also be a form of *do*, which is called a dummy operator and must often be inserted, as well:

The peaches are ripe. [positive]
The peaches are not ripe. [negative]

William has worked hard. [positive]
William has not worked hard. [negative; *not* inserted after auxiliary *has* but before past participle *worked*]

Your daughters go to college. [positive]
Your daughters do not go to college. [negative; *not* inserted after dummy operator *do*]

QUESTIONS

Declarative sentences (statements) can be made into interrogatives (questions) by switching the positions of the subject and the operator, which is the first word in the verb phrase or the dummy operator *do*:

Dolphins are clever. [declarative]
Are dolphins clever? [interrogative formed through inversion]

Storytelling has been part of our culture for centuries.
[declarative]
Has storytelling been part of our culture for centuries?
[interrogative formed through inversion]

You like cake. [declarative; could also be expressed with
a dummy operator as *You do like cake*]
Do you like cake? [interrogative formed with dummy
operator *do*]

In spoken English, sentences can also be made into questions through intonation. In writing, this can be represented as a positive statement followed by a question mark: *That's what you're wearing? You'll be there on time?*

VARIATIONS ON BASIC SENTENCE STRUCTURES

There are many possible variations on the basic sentence structures. These alternatives include sentence fragments, cleft sentences, existential sentences, and other structures in which sentence elements have been moved. These all mix up the order of the standard form. Think of them as creative devices at your disposal.

A sentence fragment is an incomplete sentence:

That's what he wanted. Money.

Incomplete sentences like *Money* are completely acceptable in fiction and nonfiction—especially in informal contexts.

Cleft sentences use *it* + *is* or *was* and a relative pronoun like *that* or *who* to add emphasis. So,

Leo saved the day.

made into a cleft sentence becomes

> It was Leo who saved the day.

Existential sentences put *there is* or *there are* at the head of a sentence for emphasis:

> Aliens are in the building.

becomes

> There are aliens in the building.

Other variations include

- Left dislocation, in which the subject gets bumped to the left and a repetitive pronoun takes its place: *Cars, they're not what they used to be.*
- Right dislocation, in which the pronoun duplicates the work of a subject and the subject is bumped to the right: *They have a lot of money, Carol and Bill.*
- Other rearrangements, such as a prepositional phrase moved to the front of a sentence: *To the mall we will go.*

Phrases

A phrase is a unit of one or more words that function as either a noun, a verb, an adverb, an adjective, or a prepositional phrase. Phrases can contain phrases within them:

Many dogs regularly enjoy the public park on Sundays.

many dogs [noun phrase]

regularly [adverb phrase]

enjoy [verb phrase]

the public park [noun phrase]

public [adjective phrase within noun phrase]

on Sundays [prepositional phrase]

Clauses

A clause is a unit that usually contains a subject and a verb. A single clause can be a complete sentence:

Jeeves slept.

Infinitives and units called participial clauses or participial phrases are also understood as clauses, even though they don't contain an explicit subject:

Perry never learned *to dance*.

Ben mastered *fencing*.

Clauses are said to be either finite or nonfinite. Finite means they contain a conjugated verb expressing a time element. Nonfinite means that the verb does not convey the time of the action. Infinitive clauses like *to dance*, in the example, are nonfinite.

Parts of Speech

Many words can function as more than one part of speech.

NOUNS

A noun is a person, place, or thing. This includes intangible things. *Thrift* is a noun. *Wrongness* is a noun.

A noun (or noun phrase) can be

- a subject: ***Milk*** *is delicious.*
- an object of a verb: *I drink* ***milk***.
- an object of a preposition: *I serve cookies with* ***milk***.
- a modifier: *Fill that* ***milk*** *bucket.*
- a subject predicative: *This substance is* ***milk***.
- an object predicative: *I call this substance* ***milk***.

A subject performs the action of a verb.

A subject predicative is the complement of a copular verb, usually *to be.*

An object predicative is the complement of the object of a transitive verb. An object predicative can be a noun (*The sheriff made him **a deputy***) or an adjective (*The sheriff made him **angry***).

The plural of most nouns is formed by adding *s*: *buildings, papers, ideas.* Nouns ending in *y* often form their plurals by replacing *y* with *ies.* Words ending in *s* often form their plurals by adding *es*: *bosses.* For irregular plurals like *children, men, deer, data,* and so on, consult a dictionary.

Possessive nouns are formed as follows:

- singular and plural nouns not ending in *s*—add an apostrophe and an *s*: *The cat's tail. The children's mom.*
- plural nouns ending in *s*—add only an apostrophe: *The dogs' tails. The kids' dad.*
- singular nouns (generic nouns and proper names) ending in *s*—Style guides disagree on whether these take an apostrophe and an *s* or just an apostrophe. Per *The Chicago Manual of Style*, it's *Charles's hat*. Per *The Associated Press Stylebook*, it's *Charles' hat*. Further, style guides contain many exceptions and special rules. Consult the appropriate style guide or choose one of two basic methods and use it consistently. The basic methods are to either always add an apostrophe and an *s* after a singular word ending in *s* or just add the apostrophe without an *s*.

PRONOUNS

Pronouns are small words that stand in for nouns. They come in different types:

- personal pronouns, subject form: *I, you, he, she, it, we, they*
- personal pronouns, object form: *me, you, him, her, it, us, them*
- indefinite pronouns: *anybody, somebody, anything, everything, none, neither, anyone, someone, each, nothing, both, few,* and others
- possessive pronouns: *mine, yours, his, hers, its, ours, theirs*
- relative pronouns: *that, which, who, whom*
- interrogative pronouns: *what, which, who, whom, whose, whatever, whichever, whoever, whomever, whosever*
- demonstrative pronouns: *this, that, these, those*

- reflexive pronouns: *myself, yourself, yourselves, himself, herself, itself, ourselves, themselves* (These words refer back to a subject—*He saw himself in the mirror*; or they are used for emphasis—*I, myself, don't like the tropics.*)
- other pronouns: the existential *there*, several uses of *it*, the substitute *one*

The existential *there* is used to emphasize new information. It moves to the subject position in the sentence. The noun phrase that otherwise would have occupied the subject position is called the notional subject: *Clowns were juggling* (*clowns* = subject). *There were clowns juggling* (existential *there* = grammatical subject, *clowns* = notional subject).

It can fill several unique roles. *It* can be used to balance a sentence that would otherwise start with a clause as the subject: *That you got a job is good news* versus *It is good news that you got a job.* This is sometimes called the "anticipatory it." Or, instead of referring to a noun, *it* can refer to a previous sentence or idea: *Leo is going back to school. It's the right choice for him.* Or *it* can create a cleft sentence, a sentence that is split in order to emphasize a particular part of it: *It is the storm that caused the power outage*, instead of *The storm caused the power outage.* Or *it* can stand in for a subject or object in a sentence where one is needed, especially in references to weather or time: *It is noon. It is raining.*

One, in formal uses, can stand in as a nonspecific alternative to a noun or pronoun: *One can visit the gift shop.* In informal contexts, *you* is often preferred: *You should check with your doctor.*

DETERMINERS

Determiners introduce noun phrases and can provide information about possession, definiteness, specificity, or quantity:

- possessive determiners: *my, your, his, her, its, our, their*
- articles: *a, an* (indefinite articles); *the* (definite article)
- demonstratives: *this, that, these, those*
- *wh-* determiners: *which, what, whose, whatever, whichever,* and so on
- quantifiers and numbers: *all, both, few, many, several, some, every, each, any, no, one, five, seventy-two,* and so on

Many determiners are also pronouns. Most possessive determiners are similar to their corresponding possessive pronouns: *her* is a possessive determiner, while *hers* is a possessive pronoun. The possessive determiners *his* and *its* are identical to their corresponding possessive pronouns. The function in the sentence determines the part of speech. In *The red Toyota is his car, his* is a determiner because it's introducing the noun phrase *car.* In *The red Toyota is his, his* is a pronoun because it's functioning as a noun phrase. In *The company made this pen, this* is a determiner. In *The company made this,* it's a pronoun because it stands in place of a noun phrase.

VERBS

Verbs convey action and states of being. Think of four main types:

- intransitive—does not take a direct object: *Jeremy **talks**.*
- transitive—takes a direct object: *Jeremy **enjoys** TV.*
- copular or linking—refers back to the subject: *Jeremy **is** nice.*

- auxiliary—a helping verb that works with past or present participles, usually forms of *have, be*, or *do*: *Jeremy **has** eaten dinner. Jeremy **is** resting.*

- modal auxiliaries—a special set that includes *can, may, might, could, must, should, will, shall, ought to*, and *would*. Modal auxiliaries address factuality: *It **might** rain.* Or they address human control or permission: *You **may** be excused.*

Many verbs have both transitive and intransitive forms: *Jeremy **knows*** (intransitive) but *Jeremy **knows** math* (transitive); *Stephanie **walks*** (intransitive) but *Stephanie **walks** the dog* (transitive).

Copular verbs convey being, seeming, or the senses: *be, appear, act, seem, smell, taste, feel, sound.* Unlike a transitive verb, which takes an object (*Dan eats **cheese***), a copular verb takes something called a complement (*Dan seems **dishonest***). Where a transitive or intransitive verb would take an adverb (*Nancy works **happily***), a copular verb takes an adjective (*Nancy is **happy***). Some verbs can have both copular and noncopular forms, depending on meaning: *Neil **acts** badly* (not copular) means Neil is an unskilled thespian. *Neil **acts** bad* (copular) means he acts as though *he is* bad. In *Fido **smells** meat, smells* is a transitive verb with the object *meat.* But in *Fido **smells** terrible, smells* is a copular verb whose complement, *terrible*, refers back to the subject. In the common expression *I feel bad*, the verb *feel* is copular, which is why it takes an adjective and not an adverb as its complement.

Verbals are verb forms that work as other parts of speech. They are

- gerunds—the *-ing* form of a verb working as a noun: ***Dancing*** *is good exercise.*

- participles—usually an *-ing, -ed,* or *-en* form. When a participle works as a modifier instead of as part of a verb, it qualifies as a verbal: *A man **covered** with bee stings came into the hospital. A child **skipping** to school is probably happy.*
- infinitives—a verb form introduced by the infinitival *to: to run, to know, to become.* Infinitives can act as subjects: ***To know** him is **to love** him.* But infinitives are also said to act as adjectives by modifying nouns (*There are many **ways to travel***) and as adverbs by modifying adjectives (*I am **happy to help***).

Verbs can be seen in terms of tense, aspect, mood, modality, and voice.

Tense indicates either present, past, or future time.

Present-tense verb conjugations are simple in English, with most verbs changing form only for the third-person singular:

I *walk* [first-person singular]

You *walk* [second-person singular and plural]

He/she/it *walks* [third-person singular]

We *walk* [first-person plural]

They *walk* [third-person plural]

Most words create the third-person singular present tense by adding *s.* Some words also add an *e: I go, you go, he goes. I pass, you pass, she passes.* Verbs that end in a consonant plus a *y* change the *y* to *ie* before adding the *s: I worry, you worry, he worries. To be* is completely irregular: *I am, you are, he is.*

Subject-verb agreement describes the use of the correct verb form to correspond with the subject. Failure to use the correct verb conjugation is considered ungrammatical:

> I am [grammatical because first-person singular subject agrees with first-person singular verb]

> I is [ungrammatical because first-person singular subject does not agree with third-person singular verb]

A past-tense verb can be a simple past-tense form or can use a past participle with an auxiliary:

> Yesterday I walked. [simple past tense]

> In the past I have walked. [auxiliary *have* + past participle *walked*]

Regular verbs add *-ed* to form both the past tense and the past participle:

PRESENT	PAST	PAST PARTICIPLE
Walk	Walked	Walked

Irregular verbs can take varying forms:

PRESENT	PAST	PAST PARTICIPLE
Speak	Spoke	Spoken
Lie	Lay	Lain
Think	Thought	Thought

Most dictionaries list past tense and past participles of irregular verbs in bold right after the main word entry: *go, went, gone.* Some dictionaries also list these forms for regular verbs. If a dictionary offers no past or past participle forms for a verb, you can assume that the verb is regular and follows the same form as *walk*.

The present participle, also called the progressive participle, is the *-ing* form, which is used with one or more auxiliaries.

PRESENT	PAST	PAST PARTICIPLE	PRESENT (PROGRESSIVE) PARTICIPLE
Walk	Walked	Walked	Walking
Speak	Spoke	Spoken	Speaking

Aspect tells you whether an action is completed or whether it is or was ongoing. The perfect aspect uses a form of the auxiliary *have* plus a past participle: *He has spoken. We have spoken.* The progressive aspect uses a form of *to be* plus a present participle: *He is speaking. We are speaking.* Some sources count simple as an aspect.

SIMPLE PRESENT	PRESENT PERFECT	PRESENT PROGRESSIVE
I talk	I have talked	I am talking

SIMPLE PAST	PAST PERFECT	PAST PROGRESSIVE
I talked	I had talked	I was talking

Mood is categorized into three types: indicative, imperative, and subjunctive:

- Indicative is the most common mood. Sentences in the indicative are usually statements, also called declaratives: *Sal washes the dishes.* Interrogatives (questions) and exclamatives (exclamations) are also categorized as indicatives, with their verbs behaving similarly to the verbs in statements.

- The imperative mood is used for commands: *Wash the dishes.* Imperatives are considered complete sentences. The subject is implied. It is *you*: *[You] Wash the dishes.*

- The subjunctive mood indicates statements contrary to fact (such as wishes and suppositions), propositions and suggestions, and commands, demands, and statements of necessity. Some uses of the subjunctive are dead or dying. In modern usage, it's most useful to think of the subjunctive as follows: In the past tense, the subjunctive applies only to the verb *to be,* and it is conjugated as *were.* The form differs from the indicative only for the first-person singular and the third-person singular.

PAST TENSE OF *TO BE*

	INDICATIVE	SUBJUNCTIVE (WISHES, DEMANDS, ETC.)
First-person singular	I *was* younger	(I wish) I *were* younger
Second-person singular	You *were* younger	(I wish) you *were* younger
Third-person singular	He *was* younger	(I wish) he *were* younger
First-person plural	We *were* younger	(I wish) we *were* younger
Third-person plural	They *were* younger	(I wish) they *were* younger

In the present tense, the subjunctive can apply to any verb. To form the present subjunctive, replace the conjugated form with the base form of the verb. (Think of the base form as the infinitive without *to.*)

PRESENT TENSE OF *TO BE* (AN IRREGULAR VERB)

	INDICATIVE	SUBJUNCTIVE (WISHES, DEMANDS, ETC.)
First-person singular	I *am*	(Smith demands that) I *be*
Second-person singular	You *are*	(Smith demands that) you *be*
Third-person singular	He *is*	(Smith demands that) he *be*
First-person plural	We *are*	(Smith demands that) we *be*
Third-person plural	They *are*	(Smith demands that) they *be*

PRESENT TENSE OF *TO TALK* (A REGULAR VERB)

	INDICATIVE	SUBJUNCTIVE (WISHES, DEMANDS, ETC.)
First-person singular	I *talk*	(Smith demands that) I *talk*
Second-person singular	You *talk*	(Smith demands that) you *talk*
Third-person singular	He *talks*	(Smith demands that) he *talk*
First-person plural	We *talk*	(Smith demands that) we talk
Third-person plural	They *talk*	(The boss demands that) they *talk*

For all these except the third-person singular, the subjunctive form is identical to the indicative form.

Modality is most helpful for understanding modal auxiliary verbs. Modal auxiliaries such as *can, may, might, could, must, should, will, shall, ought to,* and *would* deal with factuality or human control: *William can help* uses the modal auxiliary *can* to address human control. *That coffee might be decaf* uses the modal auxiliary *might* to address factuality.

Voice is either active or passive.

Active voice puts the subject of a transitive verb as the grammatical subject of the sentence: *Sam throws the ball.*

Passive voice puts the intended object of a transitive verb as the grammatical subject of the sentence: *The ball is thrown by Sam.*

PREPOSITIONS

Definitions of the class of words known as prepositions are vague and unsatisfying. Most say something like "Prepositions link nouns, pronouns, and phrases to other words in a sentence." Some people note that many prepositions—*above, on, in, around,* and so on—show physical proximity.

The best way to understand prepositions is to look at how they form prepositional phrases. A prepositional phrase is a preposition and its object. Though this fails to define prepositions, it can help you understand and identify them. Here are some of the most common prepositions: *to, with, in, on, from, at, into, after, out, below, until, around, since, beneath, above, before, as, among, against, between, below,* and *over.*

Some words can function as either prepositions or conjunctions. They include *after, as, before, since,* and *until.* For example, *before* is a preposition in *I'll have my homework done before bedtime* because it introduces a noun. That noun, *bedtime,* is its object. But *before* is a conjunction in *I'll have my homework done before I go to bed* because *before* introduces a whole clause, which is a job for a conjunction.

The object of a preposition is a noun phrase, which can be a noun or a pronoun with or without determiners and modifiers:

> Megan studied *with Joe.*

> The dogs are *at the grassiest park in town.*

The awning hangs *above the door.*

The butter is *on the wooden table.*

Mark gave the money *to them.*

The object of a preposition is said to be in object form. So any pronoun paired this way with a preposition should be an object pronoun and not a subject pronoun:

Megan studied *with him* [not] Megan studied *with he*

Mark gave the money *to them* [not] Mark gave the money *to they*

This is *between us* [not] This is *between we*

Don't throw that *at me* [not] Don't throw that *at I*

Talk *to him or me* [not] Talk *to he* or *I*

This is *between you and me* [not] This is *between you and I*

Prepositional phrases can be understood as modifiers or adverbials. Prepositional phrases can modify nouns: *the man **with the red hat***. They can modify actions: *She sings **with enthusiasm***. Prepositional phrases can also function at the sentence level, answering questions like *when* and *where*. *He will meet you **at the corner**. **In the morning**, breakfast will be served.* Or they can modify whole sentences: ***In Addition**, note the location of the exit.*

ADVERBS

Adverbs answer the questions

- when? *I'll be there **soon**.*
- where? *Bring the laundry **inside**.*
- in what manner? *Belle and Stan argued **bitterly**.*
- how much or how often? *Bruno is **extremely** busy. He is **frequently** overwhelmed.*

Adverbs can also give commentary on whole sentences. These are called sentence adverbs: ***Frankly**, my dear, I don't give a damn.* Adverbs can also create a link to a previous sentence. These are called conjunctive adverbs: ***However,** the parade was a success.*

Adverbs can modify verbs (*Mark whistles **happily***), adjectives (*Betty is **extremely** tall*), other adverbs (*Mark whistles **extremely happily***), or whole sentences (***Tragically**, the crops didn't grow*).

There also exist things called adverbials, which may or may not be adverbs:

> *Additionally*, students learn engine repair.

> *In addition*, students learn engine repair.

CONJUNCTIONS

Conjunctions connect words, phrases, and clauses. They can be divided into coordinators and subordinators.

Coordinators link units of equal grammatical status. The primary coordinating conjunctions are *and*, *but*, and *or*. Also sometimes functioning as coordinating conjunctions are *for*, *nor*, *so*, and *yet*. Some correlative expressions are also understood as coordinators.

They include *either . . . or, neither . . . nor, both . . . and, not . . . but*, and *not only . . . but also.*

> Heather likes coffee and tea. [coordinator *and* linking noun objects]

> Todd likes coffee but not tea. [coordinator *but* linking noun objects]

> Heather and Todd like coffee. [coordinator *and* linking noun subjects]

> I must go to bed now or I will oversleep tomorrow. [coordinator *or* linking grammatically equal clauses]

> Eat carrots so your eyes stay healthy. [coordinator *so* linking grammatically equal clauses]

> Eat up, for tomorrow we shall fast. [coordinator *for* linking grammatically equal clauses]

> He doesn't take the subway, nor does he take a cab. [coordinator *nor* linking grammatically equal clauses]

> Either you stay or you go. [correlative expression *either . . . or* linking grammatically equal clauses]

> Both Matt and Sam will be there. [correlative expression *both . . . and* linking noun subjects]

Subordinating conjunctions are a larger group. They include *because, if, while, although, though, until, till, as, since, when, than, before,* and *why* and longer expressions such as *even though, as soon as*, *as much as*, *assuming that*, and *even if*. Certain subordinating conjunctions that convey time, including *before*, *since*, and *until*, are also used as prepositions.

Subordinating conjunctions introduce subordinate clauses, also called dependent clauses. Subordinate clauses cannot stand alone as sentences:

> The room was redecorated. [complete sentence]
>
> Before the room was redecorated . . . [subordinate clause that is not a complete sentence]

Appendix 2

Punctuation Basics for Writers

:::::

When it comes to punctuation, professional writers should aspire to a higher standard than laypeople. A misplaced apostrophe or extra comma is much more forgivable in a casual e-mail than in a manuscript. Though no one punctuates perfectly, anyone who wants to write for publication should study the basic principles of punctuation.

Period

Use a period

- to end a sentence: *Carrots are orange.*
- to form abbreviations: *The office is at 222 Oak Blvd., near the post office.*
- to form some initialisms: *The White House is in Washington, D.C.*

Style rules vary on when to use periods with initials. Common initialisms like CIA, FBI, and LA may not have periods, depending on style.

The period is often unnecessary when an internal question mark or exclamation point appears at the end of the larger sentence that contains other terminal punctuation: *Jim wanted to ask, "Are you kidding?"*

Similarly, a sentence that ends with a period from an abbreviation or initial does not take an additional period at the end: *He visited Orlando, Fla.*

Comma

Use a comma to separate nouns, phrases, or clauses in a series. *Brett likes peas, spinach, and cauliflower. Marianne studies hard, sleeps a lot, and never watches TV.*

The comma before the conjunction *and* in these examples is called a serial comma or an Oxford comma. AP style says not to use the serial comma: *Brett likes peas, spinach and cauliflower.* Chicago style and many academics say that you should use it.

Use a comma to separate coordinate adjectives. Think of these as adjectives that modify the same noun independently: *He was a mean, ugly, immoral clown.* Note that this is different from noncoordinate adjectives: *He wore a bright red Hawaiian shirt.*

Usually, anywhere that *and* makes sense between the adjectives, you can use a comma in place of *and*: *He was a mean and ugly and immoral clown.* Noncoordinate adjectives often have a cumulative effect, and therefore *and* cannot logically replace them: *a bright and red and Hawaiian shirt* doesn't make sense as an alternative to *a bright red Hawaiian shirt.* Coordinate adjectives can often switch places without changing meaning: *He was an ugly, immoral, mean clown.* Noncoordinate adjectives cannot: *He wore a Hawaiian red bright shirt.*

The same comma rule works for adverbs. Coordinate adverbs should be separated with commas: *They easily, happily, and regularly show up to work on time.* But noncoordinate adverbs should not: *They are a very happily married couple.* Again, if an *and* would make sense, you can use a comma.

Use a comma to separate independent clauses joined with a conjunction. This use is optional, but common:

> We ate the stuffing, but the turkey remained untouched.
>
> Mark drove the bus, and Stella sat in the back grumbling.
>
> Renee had a good education, so she tried to hide that fact from Skeeter.

The comma is more likely to be omitted in short, clear sentences in which the independent clauses are joined by *and*: *I like bananas and I like oranges.*

Use a comma after introductory phrases and clauses. This use of the comma is subject to individual judgment and tastes. In general, the longer the introductory matter, the more likely a comma will help the Reader understand how the information is organized: *On Mondays Barry shows up early.* But *On the first Monday of every week in which he's scheduled, Barry shows up early.*

Use a comma with a direct address. A direct address is a name or other moniker that you call someone directly: *Hey, Jim. Listen, buddy. After you, sir. Bye, Pete.* Note that there is no comma in *Dear Jacob* because *dear* is an adjective modifying Jacob and therefore works as part of the name. But *Hello, Jacob* takes a comma.

Use a comma to introduce or set off a direct quotation. *Chuck said, "It's a great day." The docent said, "Don't touch the paintings," but Stan didn't listen.* Longer quotations are sometimes introduced with colons instead.

Use a comma to set off parenthetical information. This includes nonrestrictive clauses, appositives, interjections, and many other modifying clauses and phrases.

A nonrestrictive clause is any clause that provides supplemental information and does not restrict the meaning of a modified word. Commas or the absence of commas around clauses can significantly change meaning by signaling whether the clauses are restrictive:

> Men who like baseball are pleased. [only those who like baseball are pleased]

> Men, who like baseball, are pleased. [all men like baseball and all men are pleased]

> Fred's sister Jennifer is the youngest of the three Adams children. [Jennifer is essential information because it restricts the subject *Fred's sister*; without the name, you can't be sure which sister is being talked about]

> Fred's sister, Jennifer, is his only sibling. [Here, Jennifer is nonrestrictive information; because we know that Fred has only one sister, her name in no way narrows down— restricts—the range of possible subjects]

An appositive is a noun phrase that refers to the same thing as another noun phrase immediately preceding it:

> The president, *a decisive man*, will give a press conference.

> My wife, *Lorraine*, will attend.

> The temp, *a real go-getter*, impressed the boss.

The difference between appositives and titles is sometimes blurry:

> The U.S. Senator, Steve Stevens, signed the legislation.

but

> U.S. Senator Steve Stevens signed the legislation.

In the preceding example, we see that *the* could not logically modify *U.S. Senator Steve Stevens* because it would be akin to saying *the Steve Stevens*. So we know that *the U.S. Senator* is a noun phrase and that *Steve Stevens* is a separate noun phrase that must therefore be functioning as an appositive. Without *the*, *U.S. Senator Steve Stevens* could be a single unit with *U.S. Senator* functioning as a modifier.

The difference between appositives and noun-modifier combinations at times is purely a matter of intent:

> Her book, *The Rogue*, is a best seller.

> Her book *The Rogue* is a best seller.

In the first example, *Her book* is treated as the head noun phrase. The title is supplemental information—in this case, an appositive.

But in the second example, *Her book* is modifying the main noun phrase, *The Rogue*.

Use a comma to set off interjections. *Bombo could tell you, of course, but then he'd have to kill you.* (*Of course* is an interjection here.) *Yes, you're right.* (*Yes* here is an interjection.) *The friar, indeed, was the murderer.* (*Indeed* here is an interjection.)

The commas around interjections are often dropped when they would come too close to another comma—especially one used before a conjunction that is separating independent clauses: *Bombo could tell you, but of course then he'd have to kill you.*

Use a comma to set off other modifying phrases and clauses. In general, if an adverbial element such as a participial phrase or prepositional phrase contains parenthetical information, use commas:

> Al, being the great guy that he is, brought pizza.

> I, too, enjoy roller coasters.

> Roger, with a wink and a smile, invited Josie to his room.

> Ajax, undeterred by his enemies' skill, charged into battle.

Sometimes, the use of commas around adverbials is subject to your own judgment. For example, many say that words like *too*, *either*, and *also* should be set off by commas: *Rodney ordered lobster, too.* But this comma use is becoming less common: *Rodney ordered lobster too.*

Different styles disagree on whether *Inc.*, *Jr.*, and similar parenthetical elements in names and titles require commas. But if you use one before *Inc.* and so on, you must also use one afterward:

Warren bought shares of ABC, Inc., and Microsoft.

or

Warren bought shares of ABC Inc. and Microsoft.

but not

Warren bought shares of ABC, Inc. and Microsoft.

Dates that include the month, day, and year use commas around the year:

Dale was hired on April 1, 1982, and stayed till last year.

not

Dale was hired on April 1, 1982 and stayed till last year.

Apostrophe

Use an apostrophe

- to form possessives: *The man's house. The doctrine's flaw. The Joneses' vacation.*
- to denote omitted letters or numbers, especially in contractions: *Can't* is a contracted form of *cannot. Doesn't* is a contracted form of *does not. It's* is a contracted form of *it is* or *it has.*
- to avoid confusion, only when necessary: *The sign read, "CDs for sale."* But, *The sign read, "CD'S FOR SALE."* Here, the apostrophe is justified to make clear that *S* is not just another initial like *C* and *D. In school, Anna got Cs, Bs, and a few A's.*

Here, the apostrophe is justified after *A* because, otherwise, it would spell *As*. Some publications will bend these rules to make the writing easier on the eye: Anna got *C's*, *B's*, and a few *A's*. Publications disagree on which situations are confusing enough to justify apostrophes. For example, the *Los Angeles Times* writes *the 1980s*, but the *New York Times*'s style is *the 1980's*.

The curve of an apostrophe, if any, should open to the left, not the right. So, except in the simplest fonts, an apostrophe is identical to a closing single quotation mark, ', and should not be confused with an opening single quotation mark, '.

Quotation Marks

Use quotation marks

- for direct quotations: *The president said, "This nation will prosper."*
- in some styles, to denote words being discussed as words: *The word "jeepers" isn't as common as it used to be.*
- to denote irony or skepticism: *Yeah, that cake looks "great," Mom. I "love" the green frosting.*
- in some styles, around the titles of books, songs, movies, articles, and other compositions (other styles use italics for some of these works; consult a style guide for applicable rules and exceptions): *Smithers, a character in "The Simpsons," likes the song "It's Raining Men."*

When the matter in quotation marks could stand as a complete sentence, it begins with a capital letter: *He said, "You should leave."* When it's part of a sentence made complete by unquoted matter, the quoted portion begins with a lowercase letter. *He said he wanted me to "get lost."*

SINGLE QUOTATION MARKS

Use single quotation marks for quotations within quotations: *"They told me, 'Never come here again,'" Roy said.*

QUOTATION MARKS WITH OTHER PUNCTUATION

In standard American style, a period or comma always goes inside a closing quotation mark:

> Michelle said, "It's time."

> When Dane said, "Hello," I didn't think he was talking to me.

In standard American style, a colon or semicolon always goes outside a closing quotation mark:

> He told us the items on his "grocery list": beer and pretzels.

> He sang "Oh, Canada"; "America, the Beautiful"; and other songs, many of them anthems.

In standard American style, question marks and exclamation points may go inside or outside closing quotation marks, depending on whether they apply to the whole sentence or to the quoted matter only:

> Kojak's catch phrase was "Who loves ya, baby?"

but

> Can you believe he called me "baby"?

Also

> He said, "This is an outrage!"

but

> I'm outraged that he said, "baby"!

The same rules apply to single quotation marks:

> Jeff always says, "Why ask 'why?'"

and

> Joe said, "Have you noticed how much Jeff likes the word 'why'?"

Hyphens

A hyphen is generally less than half as long as an em dash.

Use a hyphen

- to form a compound modifier before a noun: *A sweet-talking woman.* Adverbs ending with *-ly* are an exception: *A happily married couple.* This use of the hyphen is highly subjective. No two people—not even professional editors working for the same publication—hyphenate exactly alike. The main goal of the hyphen is to prevent confusion, even momentary confusion: *I saw a man-eating lobster* versus *I saw a man eating lobster.*

- in words whose official spellings contain hyphens. The only way to be sure whether a word—especially a noun or verb—contains a hyphen in its official spelling is to check the dictionary. For example, *Webster's New World College Dictionary* says that the verb *water-ski* has a hyphen but the noun *water ski* does not.

- to attach certain prefixes and suffixes to words. There is no universal rule for knowing whether it's *co-worker* or *coworker.* Indeed, different styles advocate both. To know when to hyphenate prefixes and suffixes, consult the style guide or recommended dictionary that governs the publication you're writing for. In general, stylebooks tend to eschew hyphenating prefixes and suffixes: *nondairy, midsentence, companywide.* But they make plenty of exceptions.

Dashes

The em dash is generally more than twice as long as the hyphen. Em dashes are versatile and their uses overlap other punctuation.

Use an em dash

- to denote an abrupt change in tone or form: *Vonnegut, Joyce, Hemingway—they were all heroes in Claire's mind.*
- to set off parenthetical information: *Mr. Beasley stormed through the house—he was very angry—demanding his slippers.*
- to indicate a sudden interruption: *Will he—does he dare defy me?*
- to add emphasis: *Raul was finished by noon—he's that good.*

The en dash is less common and it's nonexistent in most newspaper styles. It's longer than a hyphen and shorter than an em dash. It can denote a range or a time span, usually meaning "up to and including" or just "to." *During Brett's time at the firm, 1998–2002, he added five branches.* The en dash can also do some of the hyphen's jobs when a hyphen wouldn't be as visually clear. For example, it can connect hyphenated items to each other: *It was a semi-public–semi-private organization,* or it can connect a multi-word term like "World War I" to another word or prefix, as in: *World War I–era planes.*

Colon

Use a colon

- to introduce a list: *Here are the items that will be served: stuffed mushrooms, beef skewers, and cheese puffs.*
- to add emphasis: *Let me tell you this: you're awesome.* AP style says that if the material after the colon forms a complete sentence, it should begin with a capital letter: *You're awesome.* Chicago style says that only if the matter introduced by the colon consists of two or more sentences should it begin with a capital letter.
- to introduce a quotation that contains two or more sentences. This use is optional. A comma is often used instead.
- to follow a direct address in correspondence: *Dear Ms. Williams:* This use is optional. A comma is often used instead.

Parentheses

Use parentheses to set off information that is less important than or somehow removed from the main passage: *I was driving an Escalade (an expensive one) when I hit the center divider.* A period goes before the closing parenthesis only if both the main text and the parenthetical are complete stand-alone sentences: *I was driving an Escalade. (It was an expensive one.) That was the day I hit the center divider.* Otherwise, the parenthetical takes no period.

Question Mark

Use a question mark with an interrogative sentence (a question): *Who moved my guacamole?* A question mark is usually considered terminal punctuation because it can end a sentence. But occasionally a question mark can appear midsentence: *When he asked, "How are you?" it was as though he actually cared.*

Exclamation Point

Use an exclamation point to denote high emotion or something exclaimed: *You monster!*

The Deadliest Catches: The Most Incriminating Errors and How to Avoid Them

:::::

Everyone makes typos. Less-experienced writers are often mortified by them, but there's no need to be. Even the most meticulous pros let a typo slip in once in a while, and the best editors and proofreaders fail to catch them all. If you misspell *led* as *lead* on occasion, no reasonable editor or Reader will think any less of you.

But there are mistakes and there are mistakes. Some are understandable. Others are code for "I'm a rank amateur."

If I see *it's* in place of *its* a single time in an article, I assume the writer made a typo. If I see it twice, that's a whole different story. That tells me—and a lot of other writers, editors, wordsmiths, and grammarphiles I know—that the writer is out of her element. She's not a pro. The grouchier among us might use words like *semiliterate* and *hack*.

So instead of agonizing over how to avoid every single typo, channel your energy into the important ones. Here is my list of iconic mistakes—ones that really do make you look bad. My selection process wasn't exactly scientific. These are just the errors that, in my experience, are most likely to inspire eye rolls and unkind thoughts about a writer's skill level.

its / it's: The possessive of *it* does not take an apostrophe: *The dog wagged its tail.* The version with the apostrophe is always a contraction of *it is* or *it has*: *It's been a fun vacation.*

there / their / they're: *There* refers to place: *Put it there. Their* denotes possession: *Their house is the green one. They're* is a contraction of *they are*: *They're good people.*

lets / let's: Without an apostrophe, this is the verb *to let* conjugated in the third-person singular: *He lets the dog out in the morning.* With an apostrophe, it is a contraction of *let* and *us*: *Let's go to the park.*

whose / who's: To show possession, use *whose*: *Can you tell me whose job that is?* The one with the apostrophe is a contraction of *who is* or *who has*: *Who's there?*

could of / would of / should of: These are always wrong. They should be *could have*, *would have*, and *should have*, or, less formally, *could've*, *would've*, and *should've*. That's because *of* is not a verb and therefore can't be used to form verb tenses. Modal auxiliaries like *could* and *should* can work this way with the main auxiliaries *have*, *be*, and *do*, but not with the preposition *of*.

where / wear / were: *Where* is a place: *Where are you going? Wear* means "to have on clothing": *Lana and Tom wear matching shirts. Were* is a past tense form of *be*: *We were so young.*

have went / have ate / other wrong participle choices: Whenever you're not sure of a correct past participle, check the main word in the dictionary. Most dictionaries list in bold the past-tense and past-participle forms of irregular verbs. Most do not list these forms for regular verbs, but some do. So, under *eat* you'll see something like **ate, eaten** in bold letters. That tells you that *eat* is an irregular verb, that its past tense is *ate* (*Liam ate a sandwich*), and that its past participle is *eaten* (*In the past, he has eaten up to four sandwiches*). Regular verbs like *walk* add *-ed* to form both the past tense and the past participle: *Today you walk. Yesterday you walked. In the past you have walked.*

accept / except: You *accept* a gift. When you *except* something, you leave it out.

compliment / complement: A flattering remark is a *compliment*. Something that completes something else, the way the right wine completes a meal, *complements* it.

affect / effect: *Affect* is usually a verb: *That doesn't affect me. Effect* is usually a noun: *What will the effect of his decision be?* Two rare synonyms defy this guideline. The transitive verb *effect* means "bring about": *The candidate promised to effect positive change.* The noun *affect* is a psychology term for emotion or a facial or bodily expression of emotion: *The patient's affect was flat.*

phase / faze: A *phase* is a stage of development. *Faze* is a verb meaning to upset or shock. *Unfazed* means unaffected.

led / lead: *Led* is the past tense form of the verb *to lead*: *He led the horse to water.* There is also the metal called *lead*, which is pronounced exactly like *led*.

then / than: *Then* is for time. *Than* is for comparison.

Computer's for sale / Merry Christmas from the Thompson's / other apostrophe errors: Never use an apostrophe to form a plural. It's *Computers for sale* and *Merry Christmas from the Thompsons*. Be especially careful with proper names ending in *s*.

grammar: Does not have an *e* in it.

About the Author

:::::

STEPHANIE DIANNI

June Casagrande is a journalist and editor who writes the weekly syndicated grammar column "A Word, Please." The author of *Grammar Snobs are Great Big Meanies* and *Mortal Syntax*, June has studied improvisational comedy with renowned troupes the Groundlings and ComedySportz. She also teaches copyediting. June lives in Pasadena, California, with her husband, four cats, and a whole lot of red pens.

Index

:::::